STORIES TO CHANGE YOUR LIFE

MIKE NOVOTNY

Published by Straight Talk Books
P.O. Box 301, Milwaukee, WI 53201
800.661.3311 · timeofgrace.org

Printed in the United States of America
ISBN: 978-1-949488-63-0

CONTENTS

INTRODUCTION

[JESUS] DID NOT SAY ANYTHING TO THEM WITHOUT USING A PARABLE.

Matthew 13:34

Even though he told it 25 years ago, I still remember my pastor's story.

It was about a man on a cruise ship who was holding an oversized bunch of beautiful balloons. He clutched the strings, not wanting a single one to float off into the sky, and marveled at the colors that formed a canopy just above his head. In fact, the man loved his balloons so much that he took them everywhere he went on the ship.

As he walked the deck to watch the sunrise, there were his balloons. As he lounged next to the pool and darkened his tan, there were his balloons. As he enjoyed a game of shuffleboard before dinner, there were his balloons.

Which turned out to be a problem.

The captain had invited all the passengers to a

party—picture a never-ending spread of food and a playlist that drew everyone to the dance floor—and the man, of course, wanted to join in the fun.

But the doorway that led into the party was narrow. Extremely so. It was barely wide enough for the man himself to squeeze through much less his plump bouquet of balloons. He tried to pull them in behind him. He tried to push them in ahead of him. No matter the angle, the man and his beloved balloons couldn't enter together.

There the man stood, watching his fellow passengers enter the party while he gripped the strings tightly in his hand. He could see the waiters carrying fresh cuts of encrusted beef to the buffet, and he could hear the joy of the guests as they ate, drank, and got merry.

The sun began to set, yet the man did not move, paralyzed by the thought of what he would lose if he just let go.

THE POWER OF PARABLES

Did I keep your attention the same way my pastor kept mine all those years ago? If you knew that the story had a moral, a point meant to guide you through life, would you put down your phone long enough to ponder what it might be? I would. I did! If you meditate on Mr. Balloons, your mind might consider . . .

- the sheer joy of being in the presence of God (aka "the party").

- the gracious invitation that God gives to us all (aka "the captain invited").
- the reality that we must repent before we are able to step into God's presence (aka "just let go").
- the sobering truth that part of us struggles to believe we can live without our sin (aka "paralyzed").

What strikes me just as much as the amount of truth packed into that story is the fact that I remember it decades later. By teaching me through a story, my pastor gave me truth without an expiration date. I've bought and tossed a lot of clothes since my teenage years, but this story has stuck with me. Stories do that, don't they?

No wonder Jesus told them so often.

As you get to know Jesus in the four gospels (Matthew, Mark, Luke, and John), you'll soon learn that Jesus loved to tell stories. Tally them up and you will find around 30 separate stories that Jesus used to teach people about the kingdom of God. The technical name for these stories is "parables."

That name comes from a Greek compound word (two Greek words that are pushed together). The Greek word *para* means "alongside." (Think of how a "para-llel" line is one that runs "alongside" another line.) The word *bles* comes from the Greek for "to throw" or "thrown." Therefore, a parable is a story that is "thrown alongside" something else.

So what exactly are Jesus' stories thrown alongside of? Answer—Invisible truths. Jesus told stories so you and I could understand invisible truths about spiritual things.

You can't see our Father when you come to him, sinful and broken, so Jesus told a story about a son who came to his father, sinful and broken, and experienced undeserved, shocking, beautiful love (parable of the prodigal son).

You can't see, even under a microscope, what happens when a little bit of God's truth gets inside your soul and goes to work, so Jesus told a story about a tiny seed that grew into a massive tree (parable of the mustard seed).

You can't see how God feels about you when you are spiritually lost, so Jesus told a story about a single sheep that mattered so much to the shepherd that he left 99 other sheep just to find the 1 (parable of the lost sheep).

You can't see how worthy God is of everything you have, so Jesus told a story about a man who found a treasure in a field and sold everything he had (with a smile on his face) just to get that treasure (parable of the treasure in a field).

That's how parables work. They are Jesus' way of helping us "see" the unseen things of the kingdom of God. So if you want to know about God, his kingdom, his Word, his love, your forgiveness, your faith, or almost anything else, Jesus has a story (or 30!) to tell you.

REVEAL AND CONCEAL

But there's one more big thing you should know about parables: Jesus used them to both reveal and conceal.

Listen to Jesus' own explanation of his teaching methods—"**The disciples came to him and asked, 'Why do you speak to the people in parables?' He replied, 'Because the knowledge of the secrets of the kingdom of heaven has been given to you, but not to them. Whoever has will be given more, and they will have an abundance. Whoever does not have, even what they have will be taken from them. This is why I speak to them in parables: "Though seeing, they do not see; though hearing, they do not hear or understand"'**" (Matthew 13:10–13).

This feels odd, doesn't it? Why wouldn't Jesus want "them" (the Pharisees and other religious leaders) to understand the kingdom of God? Doesn't he long for all people to be saved and to come to a knowledge of the truth (1 Timothy 2:4)?

Short answer—Because they didn't want to. They were too proud to. Instead of humbly coming to Jesus as their Lord, Savior, and Teacher, they dismissed him, denied him, and didn't want to submit to him. And the punishment for their pride was parables.

Jesus' parables were easy to blow off. "This hick from Galilee babbles on about fish and farmers. Why listen to him?" Thus, most of the Pharisees heard the same stories as the disciples, but they never had the humility to ask for explanations. We never find Jesus' enemies saying things like, **"Explain to us the parable of the weeds in the field,"** as the apostles did (Matthew 13:36).

In a single story, therefore, Jesus would reveal

9

God to some and conceal God from others. Humble listeners could learn more while others missed the point entirely, like a proud man clutching his balloons on the deck of a cruise ship.

MY HOPE IS THAT YOU LISTEN WITH EARS TO HEAR.

My hope is that you listen with ears to hear, that is, with a heart that really wants to follow Jesus no matter what he says or what it costs you. If you do, you will be given more faith than you have now and will end up with the "abundance" that he mentioned previously.

An abundance of grace and truth is exactly what I want today. Don't you?

MEMORABLE MESSAGES

For nearly 15 years as a pastor, I have found myself drawn back to those short stories Jesus told. As people much like you struggle with the strength of their faith, their willingness to forgive, and their desire to love people who don't share their beliefs, parables so often seem like the right page to turn to.

Passages can be hard to remember, but plots are hard to forget.

That is why I wanted to share with you a few of Jesus' stories that I have told to the people I love. The chapters that follow contain messages I have preached over the past 15 years based off the parables of Jesus.

Some of these messages were written just months ago, while others date back over a decade, but I have a hunch these words will be just as relevant for your life today. After all, the best stories are evergreen. And Jesus is the best storyteller of all.

So as your Savior often said once his parable was finished, **"Whoever has ears, let them hear"** (Matthew 13:9).

THE SECRETS TO
GROWING YOUR FAITH

CHAPTER 1

PERSEVERE IN WHAT YOU HEAR

Have you ever wondered why two people who hear the same message can end up with such different lives? If we all hear the same Word on Sunday morning, why do our Sunday afternoons look so different? If the sermon we all heard was about trusting God, why do some trust and others worry? If God commanded us all to be humble, why do some brag and others don't? If God proclaimed his unconditional love for all, why do some people feel free while others remain stuck in shame? If all the kids in a Christian school are taught the same truths, why will some grow in their faith and others take a few years off from the Word? Assuming we are all awake and our ears hear the same thing, why are our lives so different?

Or think about the differences in your own heart. Why does the same Word of God have different effects on different days? One Sunday, a passage on forgiveness moves you to pick up the phone and say, "I forgive you." Another Sunday, you intend to forgive but never get around to it. And on another Sunday, you really don't want to forgive at all. If the same heart hears the same message, why such different results? And how can we change that?

Christians have a default answer for those questions: You need more Bible. You need to go to church or open the Bible at home so you can hear what God wants to say to you. That seems like a logical answer, but that's not good enough, and I bet your experience proves it. You have met enough churchgoing people to realize that just going to church doesn't make a kind Christian. If you grew up with a dad who praised Jesus at church but acted nothing like Jesus at home, you know what I mean. While the Bible is an essential part of the Christian life, opening its pages is only part of the story. Just hearing it isn't good enough.

Jesus didn't think so either. He told a story to reveal why hearing the Word of God is not the final goal of the Christian life. And this same story explains why the same message ends up in different places for different people on different days. Jesus challenges us with this story to think beyond Sunday morning and consider what God truly wants for his children when he gives them his Word.

Look at that story with me in Luke 8:4-8: **"While a large crowd was gathering and people were coming** to Jesus from town after town, he told this parable: 'A farmer went out to sow his seed. As he was scattering the seed, some fell along the path; it was trampled on, and the birds of the air ate it up. Some fell on rocky ground, and when it came up, the plants withered because they had no moisture. Other seed fell among thorns, which grew up with it and choked the plants. Still other seed fell on good soil. It came up and yielded a crop, a hundred times more than was sown.' When he said this, he called out, 'He who has ears to hear, let them hear.'"

Simple story, right? A farmer grabs a bag full of seed and starts sowing. Some scatters on the path and is swallowed up. Some falls among the rocks and withers quickly. Some gets stuck in the thorns and doesn't make it. And some falls on good soil and brings back a tremendous crop. Same farmer. Same seed. Different results. Do you get it?

If not, don't feel too bad. Jesus' disciples didn't either. "His disciples asked him what this parable meant. He said, 'The knowledge of the secrets of the kingdom of God has been given to you, but to others I speak in parables, so that, "though seeing, they may not see; though hearing, they may not understand"'" (Luke 8:9,10).

Before Jesus explained the meaning of his story, he explained why he preached stories in the first place. Essentially, his stories both revealed the truth and concealed the truth. In other words, parables reveal the secrets of God like any good story reveals a "moral of the story" in a simple way. But for those who come with arms crossed and hearts closed, parables also conceal the secrets of God. Jesus appears to them as a silly storyteller and not a legitimate teacher. The parables become a judgment on those who don't want to listen to God.

Thankfully, Jesus' friends had ears to hear, so he revealed the meaning of the story: **"This is the meaning of the parable: The seed is the word of God. Those along the path are the ones who hear, and then the devil comes and takes away the word from their hearts, so that they may not believe and be saved"** (Luke 8:11,12). Some people are path people. They hear the Word of God, but they don't understand it (see Matthew 13:19). And they don't really want to understand it.

"Did you ask someone to explain it?"

"Well, no. I just figured it wasn't my thing."

Whenever someone hears a sermon, reads a chapter, listens to a lesson, and walks away without understanding, the devil flies down from the church rafters and has some Bible for breakfast. Those are path people.

"Those on the rocky ground are the ones who receive the word with joy when they hear it, but they have no root. They believe for a while, but in the time of testing they fall away" (Luke 8:13). Some people are rock people. They hear the Word, and they understand it. In fact, they love it.

"Jesus forgives me? God accepts me right now? The

Bible says the heavenly Father loves me even though my father didn't? Wow! That's really good news."

But then the bad news comes: Believing the Bible will cost you. You will be tested.

"So you're saying that even though she does so much for our family, she would go to hell because she doesn't believe what you believe?"

"Wait. You really think God wrote this? That a fish swallowed a guy? That God took a rib and made a human being?"

Whenever someone gives up Jesus instead of giving up a comfortable life, the seed can't take root. Those are rock people.

"The seed that fell among thorns stands for those who hear, but as they go on their way they are choked by life's worries, riches and pleasures, and they do not mature" (Luke 8:14). Some people are thorn people. The soil of their hearts is crowded, and the seed doesn't grow. The voice of God has to compete with other louder voices. The quiet voice of God says, "Give generously. I will bless you." But the voice of worry shouts, "But you can't. Not now. What if you get sick? What if they cut your hours? What if tuition goes up? You can give when you have . . . more." And the seed of generosity gets strangled.

The still voice of the Holy Spirit says, "Fathers, bring up your children in the Lord." But riches pick up a megaphone: "You don't *need* to talk about Jesus at home. That's what the church is for. And work has you crazy busy right now." Thus, the seed of faith gets smothered. Whenever there's too much going on to do the will of God, the seed doesn't grow. Those are thorn people.

"But the seed on good soil stands for those with a noble and good heart, who hear the word, retain it, and by persevering produce a crop" (Luke 8:15). Some people are good soil. They hear the Word, just like all the others, but they do something the others don't. They "retain it." They produce a crop of good works. How? "By persevering." Path people get confused and give up. Rock people get pressured and give up. Thorn people get worried and give up. But these people get confused, get pressured, get worried, and they *don't give up*. They persevere. They produce a crop **"a hundred times more than what was sown"** (Luke 8:8). Those are good soil people.

This parable reminds me of a painting I can still picture in my mind. A Lutheran church down in southcentral Wisconsin has a prominent painting just behind its altar that depicts a man who stares at you during the entire church service. It's a farmer from back in biblical times with a bag of seed slung over his shoulder. At his feet sit a few blackbirds, waiting for the seed to fall. In the background, rocks and thorns cover the soil. The farmer locks eyes with you, and his hand extends out toward you, seed flying almost out of the painting. As the pastor reads the Bible in that church, the farmer stares and throws. As the pastor preaches, the farmer stares and throws. As the people sing the Word of God, the farmer stares and throws.

And as the pastor prays, the seed falls on good soil.

So what kind of person are you? Or what combination are you right now? How often do you give in or give up, and how often do you persevere? And how can you and I become better soil?

Before we talk about becoming better soil, can we marvel at the goodness of God? This parable confronts us, doesn't it? In the last year, I went to church about 150 times (before you are envious, remember that I was getting paid for it!). I listened online to nearly 400 sermons. I read the Bible alone or with my wife over 700 times. I taught over 100 Bible classes. But I'm not bragging. I'm confessing. Based on Jesus' story, those

MARVEL AT THE GOODNESS OF GOD.

1,300 seeds ask, "Mike, what crop did you produce? For all that seed God threw at you last year, what changed? What kind of dad are you? What kind of husband? What kind of neighbor? What kind of man?" Those are sobering questions to consider.

Which is why I marvel at the perfection of Jesus. Because Jesus persevered every single time. He never gave in, and he never gave up. He knew how seasonal our obedience would be, so he persevered in our place. He was tempted by the devil with all the riches in the world, but he persevered. The thorns of his crown choked his forehead, but he persevered. Every single time Jesus heard the Word of God, that seed fell on the good soil of his heart. He received it for us. He retained it for us. He persevered for us. I can't get through one church service without some seed falling in all the wrong places, but Jesus could. And he did. And when he died and rose, he said, "I'll trade you." He traded his crop for ours, our mixture of sin and obedience for his perfection.

And because of Jesus, we don't have to wrestle with this parable alone. We are God's field. God himself is working among us. We don't have to become better soil all by ourselves. God doesn't send us out the door and say, "Be better soil!" No, instead he works within us so we can persevere. We have the power of the Holy Spirit on our side. Without his presence, this parable would crush us, but with his help, it can inspire us.

So in light of that grace, how can we become better soil? How can we take that little seed on Sunday morning and produce a crop a hundred times what was sown? The answer is as simple as it is difficult: Persevere!

To not be a path person, persevere. If you read the Bible at home or listen to a sermon and you don't understand (or aren't sure if you even want to), refuse to be confused! Ask your pastor. Ask your small group. Don't be so embarrassed that you give the devil plenty to eat. Persevere.

To not be a rock person, persevere. Pray before the "time of testing" comes: "God, I know my classmates think my faith is a crutch. Keep me strong this semester." "Jesus, I know my brother doesn't think you are the only way to God. Help me not to be ashamed of the truth."

To not be a thorn person, persevere. "Jesus, I'm worrying about this, but you said you love me and I don't have to worry." "Lord, my boss is offering a promotion, but it will choke out my time with you. Help me believe you will bless me even more." "God, this website is promising pleasure, but you say it will only end in regret. Keep me strong."

Hear the Word. Persevere. Produce a crop.

Can you imagine if you and I did? If God produced a hundred times as much in each of us? I've seen that in the members of **HEAR THE** my own church, and there have been few things more inspiring for my **WORD.** seed-sowing work. God is at work. In **PERSEVERE.** you. In me.

What if, by the power of the Holy **PRODUCE** Spirit, a little seed on forgiveness **A CROP.** would change your family and help you move past the hurt of the past? What if one sermon on God's grace would shape your image, your confidence, your identity as an accepted child of God through Christ? What if the habits you start in your home go on, long after you are in heaven, to produce generations of men and women who treasure God and his Word? Such things might seem too big to happen, but never forget what a seed can become.

God, help us to hear your Word and hold on to it!

STUDY QUESTIONS

1. Evaluate: Church sometimes does you no good.

2. Which of the soils seems most like your life lately? What made you pick that particular soil instead of the other options?

3. Some have said that Jesus' parables both "reveal and conceal" the truth at the same time. How could simple stories be easy ways to reveal God's truth? At the same time, how might simple stories be quickly dismissed by religiously educated people?

4. Study the two other versions of this parable in Matthew 13:1–23 and Mark 4:1–20, noting any additional insights that Luke did not record.

5. Look up Romans 15:5. How does God promise to help you hold on to the Word that you have heard?

CHAPTER 2

BIG FAITH STARTS SMALL

Do you ever sit down in church, look around, and wonder, "Where is everyone?" You check your watch, question if you arrived too early, and try to figure out why this gathering is a ghost town. Such Sundays can be a challenge to our faith. The energy is the opposite of Easter, and it's easy to assume that this smattering of junior varsity voices isn't about to experience anything supernatural.

The same thing can happen at Bible study. Excited to try something new, you sign up for a small group and squeeze into someone's living room on that first night. But a few people can't make it on week two. And two more drop out by week three. And they are on vacation for week four. Soon, you and the remaining few are asking, "Should we cancel?" It's hard to believe that a few folks in a fairly empty room will see a miracle. Awkward silence is much more likely.

Or maybe it's more personal. Maybe what you do

for God seems too small to matter. People love to talk about changing the world and ending injustice and reaching our community for Jesus, but your life is far smaller than that. You've invited one person to church in the past month (okay, year). You're trying to be one percent nicer at work to the guy who clutters your in-box with useless emails. You're trying to get all the kids out the door with pants on. So little about your life is "big." And that's why it's so easy to dismiss it. There are some Christians who seem "anointed," handpicked by the Father to do big things. But not you.

In American culture, we are trained to think that bigger is better. If you're buying a home, you probably want a big garage, a big backyard, and big closets. If you're looking for entertainment, you might start with the trending songs, the box office hits, the new show that's #1 on Netflix. And that's not always a bad thing. Sometimes a YouTube channel has major views because it has majorly helpful how-to videos. Big isn't bad.

BIG CAN BE DANGEROUS.

But big can be dangerous whenever it leads us to dismiss small things. In the land of bigger and better, we instinctively dismiss small things. That video has 52 views? Must be lame. This guy only has 76 followers? There's probably a reason. There are only 14 people at church? Maybe next week. If bigger is better, then, logically, smaller is not better. It's worse. And if it's very small, then it must be much worse.

But before we assume that and dismiss many of our

spiritual experiences, Jesus wants a word about what God can do with seemingly small things. Apparently, that idea matters so much that our Savior taught it through two separate stories: the parable of the mustard seed and the parable of the yeast.

Here's the first one: **"He told them another parable: 'The kingdom of heaven is like a mustard seed, which a man took and planted in his field. Though it is the smallest of all seeds, yet when it grows, it is the largest of garden plants and becomes a tree, so that the birds come and perch in its branches'"** (Matthew 13:31,32).

A mustard seed is only 1 to 3 millimeters wide. Unlike a big-old sunflower seed, the mustard seed is as small as Abraham Lincoln's ear on a penny. It's tiny, the smallest of all the seeds that gardeners used back in Jesus' day.

But don't dismiss this seed. The mustard seed doesn't just grow a bit; it grows a bunch. Bigger than your cilantro stems, bigger than your tomato plant, even bigger than the shrubs around your apartment, this seed becomes a tree! That's what Jesus said. A tiny mustard seed transforms into a tree 10 to 12 feet tall! If my calculator is correct, 3 millimeters to 10 feet is 1,000 times growth! And that is Jesus' point. If you're impressed by this big thing (the tree), then don't dismiss this small thing (the seed).

A few months ago, God did a big thing. He saved a woman's life. I'm not sure what she was going through, but she had decided the only way to escape her pain was to end her life. She even had a plan for how to do it. But then she read a little book from Time of Grace about abuse, a spiral-bound journal you could easily fit in your glove compartment. Yet God used that "seed" in a big way. The woman later emailed: "Your book made me feel loved and helped me seek a Christian counselor instead of acting on my suicide plan." That's big. This abused woman was going to end it, but instead she ended up with Jesus.

But do you know where that big blessing began? Over 20 years ago, a bunch of guys you've never met sat down at a seafood place you've never been to and said, "Let's do it!" They had just visited a Florida church that was using mass media to reach the masses with the good news of Jesus, and, despite all the unanswered questions and problems that still needed to be solved, they said, "Let's do it." And then they did it! They found a pastor they all respected, a man from Milwaukee named Mark Jeske, and a local college that would loan them some cameras. That's how, in 2001, a new program named *Time of Grace* showed up on a single television station in Milwaukee, Wisconsin.

Today, God has grown *Time of Grace* into a fairly big thing. Multiple national networks, dozens of local TV stations, millions of connections with people from all over the planet. Countless souls, like this dear sister in Christ, who are finding hope in the name of Jesus. And where did it all start? With a small group of guys gathered around a single table. Proof that we should never dismiss small things in the kingdom of God.

That's true for your story too. Maybe it would help, when your church/home/life seems too small/average/unimportant, if you told yourself, "Mustard seed moment." Maybe you could whisper it before your heart dismisses it. Mustard seed moment. Maybe we could remind each other of it before we assume that God must be somewhere else with the bigger and better types of people. Mustard seed moment.

Let's practice that—You make it to church and wonder if you're early. A few dozen people are there. There's music that won't be winning any Grammys. Your pastor isn't having his best Sunday ever. It seems small, but because the Bible is open, this is a . . . mustard seed moment. Or you're at a new job at a big place. Just another nurse on another shift. Just another teenager taking another fast-food order. Just another manager trying to manage maddening people. You do your best, pray for wisdom, try to let your light shine, but no one seems to notice. But because you are working for Jesus, this is a . . . mustard seed moment. Or you're a parent, and it's another day in the life of Mom and Dad. Making mac and cheese, buying school supplies, trying to raise a responsible teenager. No one will ask you to write a book on parenting. You start most days with, "God, help me!" and end them with, "Jesus, forgive me." But because you brought Jesus into your home, this too is a . . . mustard seed moment.

Please believe that! Tiny moments in the Word, in prayer, and in loving others are tremendously big to God. According to Jesus, that's what the kingdom of God is like.

But before Jesus moves on to another topic, he has one more story to tell. It's a lot like the mustard seed, but this parable has some extra truth sprinkled in. Matthew continues, **"He told them still another parable: 'The kingdom of heaven is like yeast that a woman took and mixed into about sixty pounds of flour until it worked all through the dough'"** (13:33). Yeast, if you don't know, is bacteria that makes bread delicious. Yeast "eats" sugars and releases tiny gas bubbles that cause bread to rise and get soft and deliciously edible. And just like a mustard seed, a little yeast goes a long way. Here Jesus says that a little yeast is mixed with **"sixty pounds of flour"** and causes the whole batch of dough to rise.

But notice Jesus' words: **"Until it worked all through the dough."** Yeast, like many ingredients, spreads *through* the whole thing. There's not a little bit of yeast here or there; the yeast is everywhere. It's not a handful of chocolate chips that you can find in a few different places but rather like the flour and sugar that find their way through the entire loaf.

That's what the kingdom of God is like. Jesus is not one little part of our Christian lives. He is not simply the teacher we listen to every Sunday or the friend we connect with every few weeks. No, Jesus spreads through everything, affects everything, changes everything.

If you're a Christian, your everything is all about Jesus. The way you think, the way you talk, the choices you make—Jesus. The way you schedule, the way you budget, the way you date—Jesus. Who you marry, how often you forgive, how much you give—Jesus. As employees, we listen to Jesus. As parents, we listen to Jesus. As sexual beings, we listen to Jesus. What does it mean to be a man? a woman? Tell us, Jesus. Where did we come from? Where are we going? What's the purpose of my life? Tell us more, Jesus. The Bible is so small that a small print edition could fit in your pocket, but its words are like yeast, spreading to every corner of your life, affecting every choice that you make. Jesus isn't part of our lives. Jesus is our life.

HE WANTS HIS WORD TO SPREAD INTO EVERY AREA OF YOUR LIFE.

Do you think that's bad or good news? Well, here's the hard part—Jesus doesn't want part of your heart. He wants all of it. He has no intention of being your part-time Lord and Savior. He wants to be your everything. He wants his Word to spread into every area of your life and raise it up to God. That will surely change you as much as yeast changes the shape of a loaf of bread. Things might be different with your sexual desires, with the way you talk about others when they're not in the room, or the way you deal with your brother's behavior. While you might be tempted to keep some parts of your life under your control, that's not how the kingdom of God works. It's like yeast. It works through all of you.

And that is such good news! When Jesus is your full-time King, he brings full-time grace. He uses his

29

authority to guarantee that you are forgiven for all of it, that you are loved through all of it, that you are alone for none of it. Have you sinned in your home against your mom? His forgiveness is there. Have you sinned in your heart against your dad? There's grace there too. You might have sinned with your gossip about your ex or with anger toward your former boss. But Jesus— don't you love this about him?—Jesus is everywhere. He doesn't forgive some things, but his forgiveness spreads through your entire soul.

And it all started so small. A little town called Bethlehem. A young woman giving birth to a little baby. A tiny town in Galilee. A man like me and you with a dozen followers and some faithful friends. One life that ended on one Friday. But when Jesus' body was put in the ground, it was like a mustard seed that would soon burst out of the ground and transform into the tree of eternal life. Jesus came back to life, and his victory over death spread like yeast, from a tiny movement in a sliver of land we call Israel through every tribe and nation and language. Today almost 2.4 billion people call upon his name, their hearts raised up to God by his unfailing love. This world might skip the small things, but we will not. We know too much about King Jesus and the way his kingdom works.

If you need more proof, just think of Charles. Years ago in England, a 15-year-old who had some religion but not a real relationship with Jesus braved a massive snowstorm to go to church. The weather that day was so terrible that he couldn't make it to his usual place of

30

worship, so he ducked into another church a bit closer to home. When Charles stepped inside, what he saw was small. A dozen people, perhaps. Even the pastor didn't make it that day, so one of the church members stepped forward and attempted to teach God's people. Little did anyone know that this was a mustard seed moment.

The preacher quoted a small snippet from the prophet Isaiah: "Look to [the Lord] and be saved." But after ten minutes, the pinch-hitting pastor was out of words . . . until he saw Charles. "Young man," he said, "you look very miserable. And you will always be miserable in life and death." Then he shouted, "Young man, look to Jesus Christ!" Then, as Charles would later tell it hundreds of times in his own sermons, "There and then the cloud was gone, the darkness had rolled away, and I saw the sun. I could have risen that moment and sung with the most enthusiastic of them of the precious blood of Christ."[1]

That sermon was the mustard seed that started Charles Spurgeon's ministry. Over the next 38 years, he would preach to more than 10 million people, write 20 million words (more than any other Christian author ever), and become known as the Prince of Preachers. But where did it all begin? With a tiny church, a teenage boy, a back-up pastor, and a single verse.

So don't dismiss your mustard seed moments. Our God loves to do big things that begin in very small ways.

STUDY QUESTIONS

1. Can you think of some of the small steps on your faith journey that have led to really big blessings?

2. A seed needs nurturing to grow. In what specific ways can you nurture your seed of faith so it can grow like a mustard seed?

3. Are there things in your life that get in the way of Jesus, times when you might hold him at arm's length?

4. In what ways can you bring Jesus into all aspects of your life, like yeast works itself through the whole dough?

5. Read the parable of the sower (from chapter 1 of this book, Luke 8:4-15). What connections do you see between that story and the parables in this chapter?

CHAPTER 3

GOD'S LOVE IS PRODIGAL

Have you heard Jesus' story about the prodigal son? Out of all the stories Jesus told, it has become one of the more frequently told in our culture. Do you know what the word *prodigal* means? Funny, isn't it? A story you may have heard since preschool and you may not even know what the title means! Well, if you don't know the word, you might miss the whole point of the story. And you might not realize Jesus' parable isn't so much about a prodigal son but about his prodigal father. I'll give you the definition in a little bit, but see if you can figure it out.

Jesus' parable begins with a prodigal request: **"Jesus continued: 'There was a man who had two sons. The younger one said to his father, "Father, give me my share of the estate." So he divided his property between them'"** (Luke 15:11,12). Can you read between the lines? The kid wants his dad's money, but he is sick of waiting for Dad to die! He wants the inheritance, and he demands it now. Can you imagine a high school senior saying, "Look, Pops, I'm sick of living with your rules and your advice and you. I want to enjoy my life instead of slowly dying here at home, but I'm broke. And you won't die. So can I just get the inheritance now so I can split?" What a prodigal thing to say! And yet, this dad does it. He takes a third of his estate, the rightful portion for a younger son (two-thirds would go to the eldest brother), and hands over what has taken him decades to gather.

Turns out it is a bad investment. **"Not long after that, the younger son got together all he had, set off for a distant country and there squandered his wealth in wild living"** (verse 13). Squandered. The Greek word means to "scatter seed." He threw his money around. The prodigal son lived prodigally. Picture a young hotshot in a red convertible with oversized sunglasses to hide his hangover streak. He arrogantly stuffs a $100 bill in the valet's shirt pocket to impress the giggling blondes in the back seat. He struts behind the bar and declares all the drinks are on him tonight. He sits courtside at every game and passes out at half of them. The paparazzi stalk him because every pic of his prodigalness is front-cover material. Wild living is good press.

But soon the prodigal budget runs into the red. He searches his pockets for a prodigal tip and comes up with pennies. He tells his buddies he can't go out for drinks unless it's two-for-one night at the corner bar. He curses at the cable station when they cut his coverage. Then the car breaks down. Then he gets fired. Then the economy tanks and the shelves are empty and the credit card is maxed and the girls stop coming by and the landlord is beating down his door. Things get bad for this prodigal son. **"After he had spent everything, there was a severe famine in that whole country, and he began to be in need. So he went and hired himself out to a citizen of that country, who sent him to his fields to feed pigs. He longed to fill his stomach with the pods that the pigs were eating, but no one gave him anything"** (verses 14-16). From prime rib to pig pods. That's a Jewish way of saying "rock bottom." Because of the Old Testament laws about food, Jews couldn't go near pigs. To eat pork was a big no-no. And to be jealous of pig food was a big uh-oh for the prodigal son.

And that's when the prodigal son does the first non-prodigal thing in the story: **"When he came to his senses, he said, 'How many of my father's hired servants have food to spare, and here I am starving to death! I will set out and go back to my father and say to him: Father, I have sinned against heaven and against you. I am no longer worthy to be called your son; make me like one of your hired servants.' So he got up and went to his father"** (verses 17-20). The prodigal knows he can either starve with the swine or take the long road home. He chooses the latter. Even though he smells like a pig and is barefoot like a first-century slave. Even though he is broke as the day he was born and knows a place back in the family is out of the question. But perhaps his dad would find it in his heart to put him on the payroll and send him to the fields for minimum wage that could put a few boxes of cheap ramen in his pantry. With few other options, the son starts for home.

We can only guess what the prodigal son was thinking as the roads became more familiar. Would his dad slam the door? give him the cold shoulder? lecture him about his loose living? demand the money back? The son might have expected a thousand things, but he definitely didn't expect his dad to be so . . . prodigal. **"But while he was still a long way off, his father saw him and was filled with compassion for him; he ran to his son, threw his arms around him and kissed him"** (verse 20). The Greek philosopher Aristotle stated, "Great men never run in public," but the prodigal father doesn't care about being great. The old man sprints. He strains hamstrings and hip muscles as his old legs leap off the back porch. The son looks up to see a cloud of dust racing toward him with his father's beaming face in the middle. The stench of a thousand unclean animals, the stink of his prodigal life, doesn't stop his dad from clutching him and kissing him and crying on his neck.

The son starts his speech: "I have sinned. I can't be your son anymore." But he doesn't get to the part about the payroll because his dad is too busy making plans. He has a prodigal party to throw for his prodigal son. **"Bring the best robe,"** he orders his servants. An amazing gift to cover his nakedness.

36

In the Bible, robes are worn by religious leaders and the saints in heaven . . . and this prodigal son. **"Put a ring on his finger,"** the father orders. To take away his poverty. **"And sandals on his feet,"** he orders. "He is no slave. He is part of our family." **"Bring the fattened calf"** (verses 22,23). Grade A, grain-fed, no steak sauce needed. And Dad gives the reason behind these prodigal plans: **"'For this son of mine was dead and is alive again; he was lost and is found.' So they began to celebrate"** (verse 24). Did you catch it? The prodigal son says, **"I am no longer worthy to be called your son,"** but his dad declares, **"This son of mine was dead and is alive again; he was lost and is found"** (verses 21,24).

Jesus' story is brilliant. Perhaps you see already why Christians love this parable. But before we apply the story, we have to finish it. Look at the interesting ending: **"Meanwhile, the older son was in the field. When he came near the house, he heard music and dancing. So he called one of the servants and asked him what was going on. 'Your brother has come,' he replied, 'and your father has killed the fattened calf because he has him back safe and sound.' The older brother became angry and refused to go in"** (verses 25-28). Here we meet the diligent, dedicated, reliable, loyal son. Just another day's work in the fields of his father until something strikes his ear. A symphony of sound. Shuffling feet and twirling dresses. Is someone getting married?

As he comes near the house, he sees the cars parked

on the lawn he meticulously mowed. Balloons are tied to the banisters he polished perfectly. And the smell of the finest beef, like the calf he fed with his own hands every single day. When the older son hears the reason for the afternoon bash, blood races into cheeks. "A party for my brother? Dad spent all this on my black sheep brother?" And the older son pouts over his prodigal father. He refuses to join the party.

"So his father went out and pleaded with him. But he answered his father, 'Look! All these years I've been slaving for you and never disobeyed your orders. Yet you never gave me even a young goat so I could celebrate with my friends. But when this son of yours who has squandered your property with prostitutes comes home, you kill the fattened calf for him!' 'My son,' the father said, 'you are always with me, and everything I have is yours. But we had to celebrate and be glad, because this brother of yours was dead and is alive again; he was lost and is found'" (verses 28-32). The prodigal father both pursues and pleads with his pouting son. "Why are you angry? Why are you jealous? Has it really been slavery to be with me all these years? Have you really suffered when all I have is yours? Should we send your brother back to the pigs, or should we celebrate? Oh, my dear son, please don't miss this moment. Our own flesh and blood was dead, and now he lives. He was lost, and now he's found."

The End. That's one of the most famous stories that Jesus ever told, a plot filled with prodigal people. Which means it is about time to answer the big question: What does *prodigal* mean? The son was prodigal. His lifestyle was prodigal. The father was prodigal. His sprint was prodigal. The robe and the ring and the sandals and the calf were prodigal. The father's heart for his pouting son was prodigal. But what does the word mean?! If you opened a dictionary, you'd find this definition: *prodigal*—"recklessly extravagant." Another definition listed—"to spend everything." Recklessly extravagant. To spend everything. Isn't that the perfect adjective for that kid? and his father? and God?

To see the connections, we need to remember the context. Why did Jesus tell this story in the first place? Whom did he see in front of him that caused him to come up with this story about a complicated family? Luke tells us: **"Now the tax collectors and sinners were all gathering around to hear Jesus. But the Pharisees and the teachers of the law muttered, 'This man welcomes sinners and eats with them.' Then Jesus told them this parable"** (Luke 15:1–3). The "prodigal sons" were coming to Jesus to hear him, notorious sinners who had experienced the rush and deep disappointment of living far from the Father. But the rule-following religious types weren't ready to celebrate just yet. Thus, Jesus told them a parable about a father who extravagantly loved both of his uniquely struggling sons.

So what do we do with Jesus' story? It might help to figure out which son is playing our part. Some of us are prodigal sons. Our sins are shocking to religious people. Drugs. Binge drinking. Abortions. Divorces.

Pornography. Infidelity. Abuse. Racism. Theft. Jail time. If that's you, notice the glorious details in Jesus' story. You might have hit bottom, ending up with only fading memories and real-life consequences after all your recklessness, and you wonder if it's too late. You sneak into the back row of church a few minutes late and leave early, afraid of too many questions about your story. You tune in to a Christian television show with the door closed, hoping that there might still be hope for a sinner like you. Part of you believes it is too late, that you have broken your Father's heart too many times, but then you look up and see . . .

God is running. Your Father in heaven is running! Not from you but toward you. And before you can find the words to say how sorry you are, he is being prodigal with you. "Bring a robe! A pure, white robe of perfection and wrap it around my child. Cover his stains and her scars with beauty that brings a smile to my face. And bring a ring so she will never forget she is spiritually rich because of Jesus, so he has a visible reminder that he has an inheritance waiting for him in heaven. Hurry with sandals so they remember that they are not slaves anymore. My love is the key that undoes the shackles. They are free now. Free to come home. Free to be with me. Free to sit at my table, hear my voice, enjoy my presence. Let's celebrate!"

IT MIGHT FEEL ODD TO CALL GOD PRODIGAL.

It might feel odd to call God prodigal, but that word

captures the shocking nature of his love. He throws a party for kids who have barely said, "I'm sorry." The world would be more cautious. The world would make you earn it. The world would draw up a contract and, perhaps, give you a second chance. But not our Father. When you come to him knowing you have sinned, he spends everything to celebrate that you are home.

Or maybe you can't relate to the sex, drugs, and rock and roll of that prodigal son. Maybe you relate more to the older son in Jesus' story. Faithful in church attendance. Diligent in volunteering. Generous in offerings. Nothing too shocking about your past. Always trying your best to do what God tells you. If that's you, Jesus' story is both a warning and a comfort.

Here's the warning—Don't miss out on grace because of your pride. Don't pout at forgiveness and look down on real "sinners" because you have "never disobeyed" God. Don't mutter and grumble when they show up to church with legal records, ripped-up jeans, and disturbing tattoos. Beware of missing out on God's prodigal love because you thought this was all about works, all about your obedience, all about you. No, it's all about grace. Your good behavior can be bad if it causes you to look down on God's extravagant love.

But here's the comfort—In Jesus' story, the father loves both of his children, the reckless one and the self-righteous one. God is still like that. He is reaching out to us all, inviting us all to join the party, to enjoy his presence. On the cross, Jesus promised paradise to a crucified thief and prayed for the forgiveness of the proud Pharisees, proof that God truly does love the world. No matter what your spiritual story, he loves you too.

There's no better title for this parable than *prodigal*. And perhaps there's no better word for God. In the Word he is recklessly extravagant in forgiving our sins. In the "new covenant" of Lord's Supper, he recklessly promises to forget the sins we have committed. And when he blesses us, his face shines extravagantly on us and sends us out into the world.

May we enjoy and imitate his prodigal love.

STUDY QUESTIONS

1. Think of whom Jesus is and what Jesus did. What was "prodigal" about him?

2. Why do you think Jesus' story contains so many ugly details about the lifestyle of the younger son? In other words, why does the Holy Spirit want you to know about the prostitutes he had been with?

3. Pride shows itself in very different ways. Some people, in their pride, go off the deep end with their sin. Other people, in their pride, seem to keep the rules but are filled with arrogance, judgment, and a disdain for grace. Which type of pride do you struggle with more? What would it look like for you to repent and turn to God?

4. The apostle Luke loves to tell the stories of the unexpected people whom Jesus loved. Page through his gospel and look at the section headings. Whose place in God's story surprises you the most? The shepherds? The prodigal son? Zacchaeus? Someone else?

5. Romans 5:20 is a timeless reminder of the power of grace. Read it, write it down, say it out loud, and thank God for his unfailing love.

THE SECRETS TO
SHARING YOUR FAITH
WITH OTHERS

CHAPTER 4

GOD'S WORD WORKS

I am bad at telling people about Jesus. That sounds so wrong to admit given my profession, but I'm not attempting to be modest. It's true. While I'm fairly confident at telling big groups of people about Jesus (preaching, teaching, writing, etc.), when it comes to those one-on-one conversations with my family or my friends, I am disappointing. It's not that I don't love Jesus; I do deeply. And it's not that I don't love people; I love them too. The problem, I have come to realize, is that I think too much about the people involved, about myself and my audience.

What if I say the wrong thing? What if I say the right thing but at the wrong time? What if I am rushing a deeply personal conversation and come off like a guy bringing up marriage on the first date? What if I burn a bridge that God is just starting to build? What if I am unwise in my approach (Colossians 4:5)? What if I need to let my light shine a bit brighter before bringing up Jesus (Matthew 5:16)? What if it's better to win them over without words before sharing the Word (1 Peter 3:1)?

When I'm not thinking about myself, I am often thinking about them. What will they say after I share my faith? What questions might they have? What objections? What baggage from a previous church experience? What intellectual arguments do they have with the Bible? What emotional ones? What if my answers aren't enough to overcome their issues?

Do you ever get stuck in that place too? If you are a Christian like me, you believe that the gospel truly is good news and you believe that good news deserves to be shared. But the process of sharing is problematic. We live in a culture where politics and religion are impolite topics for the dinner table, where too many people have negative views of the church, where "holier than thou" and "Bible thumping" and "pushing religion down my throat" are things that people mention. A lot.

Few of us know the Bible well enough to quickly answer every question that our friends have. Most of us need time to think, to find the best Bible passages, and to craft clear answers to emotional objections, but face-to-face conversations don't lend themselves to lengthy pauses like that. Texting might remove the awkward silence, but it replaces it with an agonizing lack of nonverbal feedback. When should I text? How long should I wait until I text again? Is she thinking about it or ignoring me? God, what do I do now?

Put this all together and you end up with a lot of Christians who are a lot like me. We are people who love people and love Jesus and love the idea of people meeting Jesus, but we don't love being the people to tell people about Jesus (you can read that sentence again if you need to). Maybe someone else feels better about **"making disciples of all nations,"** but not us (Matthew 28:19).

I wonder if Jesus' disciples ever felt that way. As they marched two by two into the villages of Galilee, did they ever get stuck in their own heads, doubting their own ability to evangelize and/or the villagers' desire to be evangelized? And, years later, when Jesus gave his little band of brothers the Great Commission, that mission to preach the good news to all creation, did they struggle with the same doubts? "I'm just a fisherman, Jesus." "The Greeks aren't huge fans of worshiping only one God, Jesus." "There is no way the Romans are going to agree to your sexual ethic, Jesus." "What is a guy from Bethsaida going to say to a philosopher in Athens, Jesus?" "The Samaritans, Jesus? You were serious about that part?"

Perhaps such questions, from Christians ancient and modern, are the reason why Jesus told a short story early in his ministry. It's a story about how the kingdom of God works, how the Father's vision to bring more souls under Jesus' protection becomes a reality. It's about what Christians do in that process (and what they don't). The more I study this story, the more the Holy Spirit increases my confidence to do what I long to do better and more often, that is, to talk about the Savior I love with the people I love.

Here's the story in its entirety: "[Jesus] **also said, 'This is what the kingdom of God is like. A man scatters seed on the ground. Night and day, whether he sleeps or gets up, the seed sprouts and grows, though he does not know how. All by itself the soil produces grain—first the stalk, then the head, then the full kernel in the head. As soon as the grain is ripe, he puts the sickle to it, because the harvest has come'"** (Mark 4:26–29).

"This is what the kingdom of God is like," Jesus began. Since God's kingdom is invisible, Jesus told a story about visible things, things you could easily see and, therefore, more easily understand. In this case, what happens with seeds in the ground is what happens with the kingdom of God.

"A man scatters seed on the ground." This man, who represents us, has a part to play in this story. He dips his hand into the pouch slung around his shoulders, grabs a handful of seed, and lets it fly over the fertile ground. And that's not all. **"As soon as the grain is ripe, he puts the sickle to it."** When the harvest comes, the man is back in action, swinging his sickle with the same hands that sowed the seed. He has a part to play in this process.

But notice what happens in between the sowing and the reaping. The "man" and his work are barely mentioned. We don't hear much about what he does during the months after the seed has snuggled into

48

the soil. All we know is that **"he sleeps"** night after night and **"he gets up"** day after day. If he's the eight-hours-per-night type, this guy spends a third of this story sleeping! Doing nothing. Not tending or watering or watching. Nothing.

And don't miss his ignorance: **"The seed sprouts and grows, though he does not know how."** This sower is not a scientist with a thorough understanding of the complex biology squeezed inside the crusty seed. Ask him exactly how that tiny thing turns into the tall grain that he will harvest for his daily bread and he will admit, "Um . . . I don't know."

Jesus even adds this telling line: **"All by itself the soil produces grain."** All by itself! The man is completely excluded from this part of the process. In other words, if this were a movie, the "man" would not be an A-lister like Tom Hanks or Chris Pratt but a no-name actor whose name zips by during the closing credits.

If the sower isn't the star of this show, who is? The seed. While the man is sleeping, **"the seed sprouts and grows."** The seed bursts from its shell, reaching out its roots, sending up its sprout, drinking in the moisture, and soaking up the sun. While the man is snoring away at home, the stalk is making its slow vertical journey, producing the head that will hold the kernel that will eventually fill his belly. In a time-lapse film from sowing to reaping, the man is barely there, yet ripened grain grows nonetheless. It works even when he doesn't.

Jesus' story reminds me of my backyard. One day

I was mowing the grass and weeds that I call my yard when my nostrils noted a fragrant scent in the air. I looked down and saw . . . mint. A few fully-formed mint leaves were standing proudly amongst the grass. And, while they appeared to be the only inmates to break out of the walls of my garden prison, they weren't alone. Inside our little fenced-in garden was enough mint to make mojitos for most of Mexico! Easily hundreds, probably thousands, of fresh mint leaves were waiting to be plucked and chewed (or muddled and stirred), which might make you question why we planted so much in the first place. But we didn't. In fact, we didn't plant anything in our garden that year. Not a single seed. Yet a single

THE CREATOR, mint plant put in the ground a
WHO MADE HIS few years ago had grown despite
our inactivity and our ignorance.
WORLD WORK, My wife, Kim, and I did play our
WENT TO WORK. part—we planted the original plant—but then we went to bed and woke up a few hundred times. That's all. Meanwhile, the Creator, who made his world work, went to work even when we didn't.

"This is what the kingdom of God is like." Jesus wants you to know that. The Word of God is like mint. God's message is minty. Before you freak out about sharing your faith or anxiously bail on a chance to talk to your friend about Jesus, remember this story. Remember what you do in this process and, just as important, what you don't do. Remember that God's

Word works even when you don't.

In other words, sharing the Word is not like writing an English class essay. When you go to bed with 427 words finished, you wake up with 427 words. When you take a brain break at 793 words, you come back to your laptop with 793 words. The work, in other words, only gets done when *you* work. It depends on *you*. The number of words doesn't grow unless you make it so.

But God's Word is not like that. Less like that essay and more like my mint, the message about Christ is infused with its own power, a divine nature that allows it to sprout when you're taking a nap and grow when it's not even on your mind. Planting that seed is indeed your role, but that seed goes to work in ways we can't entirely understand. Just like a seed planted in the soil.

This is what God has always wanted us to know. The prophet Isaiah spoke for our Father when he said, **"As the rain and the snow come down from heaven, and do not return to it without watering the earth and making it bud and flourish, so that it yields seed for the sower and bread for the eater, so is my word that goes out from my mouth: It will not return to me empty, but will accomplish what I desire and achieve the purpose for which I sent it"** (Isaiah 55:10,11).

The writer to the Hebrews agreed when he wrote, **"For the word of God is alive and active. Sharper than any double-edged sword, it penetrates even to dividing soul and spirit, joints and marrow; it judges the thoughts and attitudes of the heart"** (Hebrews 4:12).

Jesus' half-brother James taught, **"Humbly ac-**

cept the word planted in you, which can save you" (James 1:21).

And the apostle Paul promised, **"Faith comes from hearing the message, and the message is heard through the word about Christ"** (Romans 10:17). This Word about Jesus is not a lifeless thing that needs your constant attention. It is "alive and active," able to accomplish what God desires, convicting people of sin and saving them from guilt. It first creates and then strengths faith in a process that we don't entirely understand. What a Word!

So what does this all mean for timid evangelists like us? It means that God's Word will work in ways we don't grasp just yet. That's what a young man named Chris found out. Pastor Andy Stanley once mentored a passionate young man named Chris who desired to share the gospel with his entire high school before his graduation day. His intentions were pure, and his drive was genuine, but, sadly, doors didn't open as Chris prayed they would. Graduation day came and went, but his goal remained unreached. There were so many classmates who never heard the message about Christ from Chris' lips.

But the Word was working even when Chris was not. The year after Chris' graduation, his high school hosted their annual event about the dangers of drinking and driving. (Picture hundreds of teenagers sitting on gym bleachers hearing gory tales of lives lost.) The school principal had invited Mark, a current student, to share his life story, since he had been a heavy drinker and drug user before experiencing a shocking change of heart during the previous school year. Mark agreed, standing at a microphone in front of the standing-room-only crowd of his peers, telling them all about how much he used to drink and how much he hated everyone at their school when he had moved the prior year from Miami. No one breathed as Mark poured out all the ugly of his story.

What changed in his life? The short version of what Mark shared went like this—"One day a guy named Chris invited me to his house. I told him all about my life. I told him how much I hated everybody. He listened. And then he told me Jesus loved me. He explained how Jesus died on a cross for my sins. My life changed. I still have my struggles. But now I don't have to face them alone. If you have any questions about anything I've said, I would be happy to talk with you afterward. Thank you."

As Mark made his way back to the bleachers, the gym erupted in applause. The whole student body— freshmen, sophomores, juniors, and seniors—joined in cheering Mark for his bravery and his transparency.[2] Did you catch that? The *whole* student body. A year earlier Chris had prayed to share the good news with the whole student body. And it worked! Just not when he was working. **"The seed sprouts and grows, though he does not know how. All by itself the soil produces grain"** (Mark 4:27,28). Minty, isn't it?

That same "all by itself" nature of God's Word hasn't changed. The message that I long to share with

53

others is just as power packed as it was when Chris told it to Mark. It is just as potential filled as when the apostle Peter spoke it to thousands on the Day of Pentecost. Same Word, same Spirit, same promise. **"The Word of God is alive and active"** (Hebrews 4:12).

So here's God's challenge for people like you and me: When you're afraid it won't work, remember how the Word works. Let me repeat that just in case you didn't underline the most important sentence in this chapter: *When you're afraid it won't work, remember how the Word works.* When you're afraid that you're not competent or they aren't the "type" to believe it, remember how the Word works. It is a seed that has supernatural power. It is full of the Spirit and of life, the same Spirit that can break through the soil of hard

REMEMBER HOW THE WORD WORKS.

hearts, the same life that gave you life when you were dead in your sins. Before you psych yourself out of evangelizing, think about the Word. Recite the words of Isaiah chapter 55 or Hebrews chapter 4 and remember you are not writing an essay; you are sowing a seed.

That won't guarantee the "grain" of every soul will be saved or every life changed. As we learned in chapter 1 of this book, Jesus told other stories about hard soil, hungry birds, blazing sun, and choking thorns to remind us that just as God's Son didn't see "success" with every sermon, we won't either. Even bold prophets and eager apostles knew the sting of spiritual rejection. Yet they also saw fruit. Sometimes many people believed them. Sometimes just one person. Sometimes they witnessed lives changed during their time in town. Sometimes it didn't happen until long after they had left. But the Word worked.

It still does. I've witnessed it. A few years ago, a teenager named Brandon moved in with his grandmother, who was a member of our church. One of the conditions of him living with her was joining her on Sundays for our church services. Brandon agreed, but, being the clever kid that he is, pointed out that he never specified *where* he would be in the building during those Sundays at church. That's why he found a couch in the church lobby, pulled out his phone, stuck in his earbuds, and scrolled YouTube while I preached the gospel in the nearby sanctuary. Not exactly how his grandma planned it . . .

But one day, for some unknown reason, Brandon took his earbuds out and listened as the lobby speakers carried the message in his direction. A few Sundays later, for some unknown reason, he agreed to spend the service up in the technology booth with some of our staff who ran sound and lights. A few Sundays after that, for some unknown reason, he moved down to the front row of our church and leaned in as I talked about Jesus. I remember him sitting there, barely blinking, ignoring his phone, hanging on every Word. I remember Brandon sometimes fist-bumping me as I returned to my chair after the sermon, sometimes just hugging me after the service was over. Something was happening in Brandon's heart, though I couldn't see it or entirely understand it.

We met for coffee a few times, where Brandon shared a worldview that I didn't share with him, a belief system that, honestly, I didn't know how to talk him out of. Turns out I didn't need to. As the months passed, Brandon's words had a new sound to them, new words that flowed up and out of a heart that was being made new. He began to talk about Jesus as "the perfect example of love" and, even more, "as God's Son." He repeated to me the good news that I had preached to him, news that he didn't just know in his head but also believed in his heart. Brandon didn't claim that his life was perfect or that his struggles with sin were over, but he did profess something new. Or Someone.

Just after his 19th birthday, Brandon was baptized in the name of the Father, the Son, and the Holy Spirit. The angels in heaven erupted in praise even more than our church family on that special Sunday. That is saying a lot, because we celebrated a lot!

How did that happen? How did a kid who wanted nothing to do with his grandma's God end up worshiping him by her side? I honestly don't know. I wouldn't have predicted it. But maybe that's why Jesus once told a story: **"Night and day, whether he sleeps or gets up, the seed sprouts and grows, though he does not know how"** (Mark 4:27).

STUDY QUESTIONS

1. On a scale of 1 to 5, how would you rate yourself at sharing your faith and why?

2. When sharing your faith with others, do you put a lot of pressure on yourself to say the right words or know the right Bible passages? Based on the parable in this chapter, who's at work when God's Word is spoken?

3. Explain: God's Word is minty.

4. What encouragement does this story give you regarding your own spiritual growth?

5. What can you do in your life, and in the lives of others, to create conditions where the Word of God will grow?

CHAPTER 5

LOVE LOOKS. LOVE GOES. LOVE GETS.

Last fall my 8-year-old daughter dressed up like an 80-year-old woman. She got on stage with 50 other kids dressed as gray-haired, walker-wielding great-grandparents, and they all sang together. The song they sang was about the "kids" in the world today and how there's something wrong with them! Ever heard that song? It comes from the 1960s musical *Bye Bye Birdie*, but the lyrics are timeless because every generation says the same thing about the generation after it—What happened? If you graduated during the 70s, your hair and bell-bottoms probably drove your grandparents nuts. If you were a child of the 90s, your dad might have vented about your *Street Fighter II* addiction or your depressing Nirvana music. If you're a millennial, your mom doesn't get why you only talk via text. And if you're under 24, you wonder why anyone would text when you can Snapchat.

Those in that last generation were born between 1995 and 2012. It's the latest generation to get an official name—Generation Z. Generation Z is made up of grade-schoolers, high schoolers, college students, and young adults—24 percent of the American population. Gen Z might be you or your younger sister or your nephew or your son or your neighbor or the person sitting next to you in church on Sunday. In fact, I'd love for you to write down the name of someone from Gen Z whom you know/love so this chapter is as personal as God wants it to be.

Like every generation, these "kids" are different. Not better or worse, not good or bad, just different, like you were probably different from your parents. Dr. Jean Twenge, a psychology professor from San Diego State, recently compared Gen Z to the rest of us. While every person is obviously an individual, she noticed a few striking trends among the youngest Americans. They like the *internet*—the average Gen Zer spends six hours on social media, apps, and the internet each day. They sleep within arm's reach of their phones and use them to connect with friends. They're also *independent*. They're much less likely to be a die-hard Democrat or a hard-line Republican or committed to any Christian denomination. They're *inclusive*; they've seen and read of the damage done to minorities in previous generations and have no plans to repeat the past. Many are *in no hurry* to start "adulting," with fewer high schoolers getting a driver's license and fewer 20-somethings getting married or having kids. Many are also *insecure* (mental health is a massive struggle), anxious about what others think and afraid that they won't make enough money to pay back their immense student loans.[3]

Before I get to one final point, what do you think of Gen Z? Are you fascinated? frustrated? grateful? fearful? One of the biggest dangers for us older folks is pride. We wonder why the next generation can't be like us. You know, perfect. Yeah, right. Jesus warned about this kind of pride, especially among religious people and specifically with kids. **"Do not despise one of these little ones,"** Jesus commanded his disciples (Matthew 18:10).

But there's something else you should know about Gen Z. They are, according to Dr. Twenge's data, *irreligious,* the "least religious generation in US history."[4] One in four high school seniors and one in three college students don't ever go to church, don't ever pray, and don't even believe in God. In my community from 2000 to 2010, those unaffiliated with any church of any religion grew by 681 percent.[5]

For many Christians, this is at the top of our prayer lists. We pray passionate prayers for our kids, grand-kids, nieces, nephews, younger brothers, classmates, and peers. We want the kids to stay close to Jesus and his Word and his people. And, for those who have wandered away, we pray they come back.

But what if there was something else we could do besides just stay and pray? What if God was calling us to something bigger, more challenging, but more beautiful? Because that's what Jesus taught his disciples to do. In Matthew chapter 18, Jesus taught his longest sermon ever about the next generation (I would encouraged you to pause here and read it if you have time). "Don't sin against the kids," he insisted. "Don't look down on the kids," he warned. And then Jesus said something famous—he told the parable of the lost sheep. It's a short story you might've heard but might not have known that it was, at least in Matthew's gospel, about the next generation.

Check out Jesus' words: **"What do you think? If a man owns a hundred sheep, and one of them wanders away, will he not leave the ninety-nine on the hills and go to look for the one that wandered off?"** (Matthew 18:12). What do you think? Jesus wants to know your answer because it will determine how you treat your neighbor. If you got a 99 percent on your chemistry final, would you think it's a good grade? If you retained 99 percent of your clients from the past year, would you think it's good business? If you ended the day with 99 percent of your flock, would you think it's a good church? If 99 percent of the kids stuck around and 99 percent of the chairs were occupied on Sunday, would that be good? What do you think?

Think of it like this family from my church. Brian and Amanda have five sons: Logan, Parker, Myles, Lincoln, and Sawyer. Can you imagine if they went on vacation and came home with only four sons in the back of the oversized white van they drive? If Logan was lost, would Brian be cool with that? Would Amanda shrug and say, "Well, we still have four. That's more than most families!" What do you think? No! That's not just a stat; that's her son!

And that's how God feels about the Gen Z name you wrote down. The one teenager in your family. The one guy on your team. The one girl from your dorm. That person is a soul God created. That person was someone on Jesus' mind when he went to the cross. That is a person the Spirit is reaching out to. That is a sheep the Shepherd can't stand to lose.

But sometimes sheep wander. We're all prone to wander. Jesus didn't say in this verse that we run away or rebel but that we wander. Like a sheep that sees a good patch of green grass just over there . . . and then another . . . and then . . . we can end up in a place far from the flock, far from the Shepherd. A place we never planned to be.

If you're fairly young, wandering will be one of your greatest temptations. And I feel for you. Because you face some temptations I didn't growing up. Like economic insecurity. College is insanely expensive. So you pack in the AP courses, the college credits, and work weekend shifts to save up. And you're not against church; it's just that it feels like you need a few extra dollars more urgently than you need a few extra services. Then there's the internet. You know more of the ugly parts of organized religion than your grandparents. You've read the stories of hypocrisy, abuse, cover-up. You're like kids who witnessed a bad divorce and now are nervous about marriage. You've seen the ugliest parts of church, and I don't blame you for wandering from these gatherings for worship. And then there's your friends. They're probably way more diverse—ethnically, spiritually, sexually—than your grandma's friends. Sometimes that challenges the teachings you grew up with about what God is for and what he is against. For you, the church's stance on homosexuality or Buddhism are not hypothetical but are instead connected to people you know and love. I get it. I get why younger generations wander.

So what will the rest of us do when it happens? When that name you wrote down is working and not worshiping on Sunday. When she has a bad experience and goes spiritually independent. When they start caring more for how their friends feel than for what their Father feels, what will we do? Just complain about the kids? Just stay and pray? Just wish they wouldn't wander?

THE GOOD SHEPHERD ...
GOES AND GETS.

No, listen again to Jesus: **"Will he not leave the ninety-nine on the hills and go to look for the one that wandered off?"** The Good Shepherd doesn't stay and pray. He goes and gets. He leaves and looks. Picture him at the end of a hard day. The sun is going down. The sheep are lying down in the pen. "97, 98," the Shepherd counts. "99 . . . wait." He counts again. Then again. He squints out at the field, looking for a patch of white wool. Nothing. So what does he do? He leaves.

He looks. It'll be work. He doesn't have an F-150 with heated seats. He will be forced to go down into the gloomy valley, climb up the rugged mountain, plunge into the shadows, prepare to fight any wolf who took away his one. That's what love does. Love looks. Love goes. Love gets.

I won't lie to you. Finding wanderers and turning them into worshipers will not be easy. Things have changed. The cultural ideas that "I really should get back to church" and "Church is a good thing" and "Christians are admirable people" are dead. When people find out I'm a Christian pastor, they're not impressed; they feel awkward. The internet and shows have taught them what people like me are like: money-hungry hypocrites who cheat on their wives, hate gay people and immigrants, and have sworn a blood oath to the Republican party. So it takes time, lots of time, to prove them wrong, to go and get them to change their minds. It takes a lot of listening, a lot of love. It takes years of building trust, of opening a door. This will take time. We can't squeeze going and getting into those small slots in our schedules. It might take years of showing how Jesus does make a difference in life and in suffering and in pain. We can't hide, and we can't hate. We have to go and get. Not with some evangelistic agenda. But with the goal to show them God's love.

So what would looking be like for you? What would love do? Maybe today you could start to think about what looking would look like? What would be the best way to show your love to that one? What would you say? What would you do? When would you talk? How could you connect? In an anxious generation, how could they see, up close and personal, the power of knowing the God who runs the show? How could you let your light shine?

Because something amazing might happen: **"And if he finds it** [the Good Shepherd finds his wandering one], **truly I tell you, he is happier about that one sheep than about the ninety-nine that did not wander off"** (Matthew 18:13). Happy. That's how he feels. Insanely happy. How else could you feel when someone who matters so much comes home?

That's how I feel about Lacey. Lacey is a young woman who came to my church a while ago and said I could share her story. Lacey had some spiritual connections growing up, but life got busy and she wandered. She didn't really know Jesus or trust in God. But now you should see her. Lacey has her roots deep into Jesus. She gathers with us on Sundays and does life in a small Bible study group and grows in the Word at home and gives generously and goes to let her light shine. And she has spiritual fruit. More peace than in the past. More love for her family. More joy because of Jesus. And that makes me so happy. Yes, the other 99 who haven't wandered make me happy too, but there's something so good about the 1.

What if this year, your "one" became the next Lacey? Could you imagine that for a moment? What if a year from now that person was in church with

65

you? What if you heard that person's voice joining yours in the Lord's Prayer? What if you saw that person's progress on the Bible App and liked his or her highlighted passage with the happiest emoji face you could find? What if he got baptized? What if she came back to Jesus? That could actually happen. That has happened. That does happen when we love and look, when we go and get.

Like Jesus did with us. He concludes in Matthew chapter 18, **"In the same way your Father in heaven is not willing that any of these little ones should perish"** (verse 14). In the same way, just like that shepherd would go and get the one, God did too. He wasn't cool with 99 Christians. He cared about the wandering 1. He cared about you. You were not some number on God's spreadsheet. You were a name, a name he knew, a face he couldn't stand not to see. That's why Jesus didn't stay and pray in heaven. No, he loved enough to come look. He left heaven, he lived perfectly, and then left the tomb empty. Jesus loved you enough to die for you, to forgive you, to invite you. And he loved you enough to nudge your mom or your brother or your boyfriend or your best friend to love you, to invite you, to tell you about God's unconditional love. Because God is love. Because that Love looked.

That's what musician Cory Asbury figured out. Raised by a far-from-perfect father, he didn't understand what God the Father was like. Probably angry at him. Disappointed. Distant. But in 2010, something changed. Cory had a son. When he held his baby in his arms, he felt a love like nothing he had felt before. An overwhelming feeling. And he realized that his kid hadn't done anything, hadn't earned it or deserved it, but he still felt it. He finally understood the Father's heart. The heart that would do anything—climb a mountain, kick down a wall, plunge himself into the darkness, risk it all—for the sake of just one. So one day Cory Asbury wrote a song you might have heard: "Reckless Love." It's all about the overwhelming, unending, reckless love that God has for us. We don't deserve it, but he gives it to us freely. When Cory wrote the song, some Christians wondered if *reckless* was the right word to describe God's love, but what other word would describe a Shepherd who would sacrifice his safety, his comfort, his life? **YOU AND I** A Shepherd who would lay down everything for the sake of just one who wandered?

WANDERED,

This is our story. You and I wandered, and Jesus found us. **AND JESUS FOUND US.**

It made him so happy that the angels in heaven threw a party. That's the story we want for the next generation. To be overwhelmed by the reckless love of Jesus and the Father's gracious heart. So let's go and get. Let's look. Let's love so another generation would love our Savior Jesus.

STUDY QUESTIONS

1. When we think of the next generation, we often fall into the trap of pride in our own and disdain for the younger. Proverbs 11:2 says, **"When pride comes, then comes disgrace, but with humility comes wisdom."** How does a prideful mindset get in the way of actions that you can take in humility and wisdom?

2. Write down the name of one person you know in Generation Z. Now look at Matthew 18:12–14 again. With that name in mind, explain how 99 percent can seem like a failing grade.

3. Describe what a church looks like that refuses to leave the 99 to look for the wandering 1. Why is the "stay and pray" strategy so tempting for Christians?

4. Read over Luke chapter 15, Jesus' famous teaching on the happiness God feels when lost things/people are found. Note two things you learn about the heart of God from these verses.

5. Take the first step in "leaving and looking" for someone you know who has wandered from the Christian faith. This might be a text, a coffee, an apology, or anything that expresses your genuine love for them as a person.

THE SECRETS TO
LIVING A LIFE OF FAITH

CHAPTER 6

BE SPIRITUALLY SMART

"You shouldn't say the word *stupid* in a sermon." That's what a mother of four told me after church. I had just dropped the S-bomb in my Sunday message, and she confronted me about it. "I teach my kids not to say that at home, and then they hear it at church!" She had a point. I wouldn't want my kids pushing back on me, "But our pastor says it!"

But in my defense, God said it first. Not very often, but there are four spots where he chose to put *stupid* in the Bible. Here's the most famous: **"Whoever loves discipline loves knowledge, but whoever hates correction is stupid"** (Proverbs 12:1). Whoever hates being corrected, critiqued, called out is stupid.

I don't think that's going to be my new life verse, because I think God is calling me stupid. I don't love correction. I'm sure you don't like it either. I don't print and frame critical emails. A woman once wrote me a letter entitled, "95 Complaints About Pastor

Mike." I didn't love that. Does that make me stupid?

On the other hand, I get the point, because it takes correction to get better at anything. Whether it's shooting threes or baking cakes or caring for patients, we all need advice, right? And I suppose that's true spiritually. We'd all like to be more patient and more loving and more self-controlled. And sometimes we never see how to grow in those areas until someone writes an honest email or has a heart-to-heart with us. So spiritually smart people listen—even love—that feedback. Whoever wouldn't want to be more patient or kind or loving or faithful would obviously be . . . well . . . stupid.

That begs some really fascinating questions about your spiritual smartness. Like who do you let correct you? How often do you ask for correction? When do you invite your parents (or your kids!), your friends, and even your critics to make you spiritually smarter?

God cares a ton about those questions because— believe it or not—a person's biggest spiritual problem is not sin. It's being stupid. Sin will not keep you out of heaven (or it would be empty!). Being stupid will. Hating correction. Avoiding conversations. Refusing repentance. That's eternally stupid.

To prove it (and to encourage spiritual smartness), I want to share a sobering story that Jesus told the Tuesday before he died. It's a parable that proves the ancient proverb that I quoted earlier. **"Jesus then began to speak to them in parables: 'A man planted a vineyard. He put a wall around it, dug a pit for the**

winepress and built a watchtower. Then he rented the vineyard to some farmers and moved to another place'" (Mark 12:1). This rich guy plants a massive grape garden, finds some renters, and moves away. We might say, "A man built a beautiful duplex, moved in, rented out the other half, and took his wife and son on a six-month trip around the world." So far, so good.

"At harvest time he sent a servant to the tenants to collect from them some of the fruit of the vineyard" (verse 2). Since direct deposit has yet to be invented, this first-century owner has to find another way to collect the rent. And since he's out of town, he sends a servant just like the duplex owner might send his buddy to stop by on the first of the month to pick up the check. And notice the rent: "some of the fruit." He's not demanding all the fruit or even most of the fruit. He just wants some of the fruit. He's a generous man and wants the renters to enjoy the vineyard too.

But things get stupid in verse 3: **"But they seized [the servant], beat him and sent him away empty-handed."** Whoa. The renters shove the owner's friend off the front porch. They kick him as he tries to gain his footing. When he tries to stand up for himself, one renter slaps him across the face, wraps five fingers around his throat and threatens, "Get out of here!" He does, staggering back to his car without a check in his hands.

The landlord hears the disturbing news, so he tries again. Verse 4: **"Then he sent another servant to them; they struck this man on the head and treated him shamefully."** The wretched renters burst through the screen door before the first knock. They slap the man upside the head. Surround him. Spit in his face. Mock him as fear floods his eyes. Verse 5: **"He sent still another, and that one they killed. He sent many others; some of them they beat, others they killed."** No! Who would do that? Multiple counts of abuse, of murder? For a little extra fruit? Who would be that stupid?

Verse 6: **"He had one left to send, a son, whom he loved. He sent him last of all, saying, 'They will respect my son.'"** No, no, no . . . don't do that. On the other side of the world, the landlord is out of options. But his son isn't a servant. He's a member of the family. They'll respect that. They have to. So he drives his son to the airport and kisses him goodbye.

Verse 7: **"But the tenants said to one another, 'This is the heir. Come, let's kill him, and the inheritance will be ours.'"** The wretched renters hatch a wretched plan. And then they actually do it. **"So they took him and killed him, and threw him out of the vineyard"** (verse 8). They murder the son and dump his body back in the woods. Before the corpse is cold, they crack a few beers to celebrate their new status as owners of the vineyard.

Jesus pauses. He looks around at the stunned crowds and asks, **"What then will the owner of the vineyard do? He will come and kill those tenants and give the vineyard to others"** (verse 9). Exactly. You don't get away with murder. You don't steal the owner's stuff and live happily ever after. Justice comes tomorrow if not today.

73

Jesus turns to the crowds and asks, **"Haven't you read this passage of Scripture: 'The stone the builders rejected has become the cornerstone; the Lord has done this, and it is marvelous in our eyes'?"** (verses 10,11). This is a lyric from an ancient worship song called Psalm 118. It's about a stone that the construction workers called worthless. But it ended up being the cornerstone, the most important stone, the essential stone for the whole project.

Huh? What do the stone rejectors have to do with the wretched renters?

Jesus' audience knows exactly what he is trying to say. And, in their stupidity, they hate him for it. Verse 12: **"Then the chief priests, the teachers of the law and the elders looked for a way to arrest him because they knew he had spoken the parable against them. But they were afraid of the crowd; so they left him and went away."**

Get it? The religious leaders were like the renters. God gave them a sweet place to live and serve, the temple in Jerusalem, but it wasn't enough for them. Because when God sent his servants, prophets like John the Baptist, to collect the rent (the fruit of love and humility and compassion and forgiveness), they beat them down with their insults. And when God sent his Son, the Son he loved, they planned to murder him. And then they did. To put it another way, God wanted to build his church on Jesus, the cornerstone, a marvelous plan to those who believe, but the "builders" rejected him and tossed him on the junk pile of Calvery.

If you had to pick one word to describe those rent-ers/those builders/those religious leaders, what would it be? How about . . . *stupid*? Servant after servant after servant after servant came to collect, to correct their behavior, but they hated it. They hated it so much they would beat and shame and kill. They hated it so much they would crucify the Father's only Son.

So what does that have to do with you and me? Is it an encouragement to pay your rent on time? No, this is something much more, something that has to do with all of life, with everything spiritual. Maybe we could think of it like a fresh, delicious pizza. Let's imagine that your friend has a pizza. He is so generous that he has decided, free of charge, to give you this pizza. Even better, he is cool if you eat some of his pizza. Not just a bite or two but slice after slice. But he has one request—that you share some of this pizza with others. Seems more than reasonable, right? What

EVERYTHING AND EVERYONE IN THE WHOLE WORLD BELONGS TO GOD.

would be unreasonable, what would be stupid, would be to scream at your friend, "This is mine!" What would be crazy would be to go all Jackie Chan on anyone who steps up and takes some of YOUR pizza.

Get it? See if this passage helps. Psalm 24:1 says, **"The earth is the LORD's and everything in it, the world, and all who live in it."** Everything and everyone in the whole world belongs to God. God is the owner, the Maker, the Creator. But God the Father is so good, so generous, that he gives. He gives us his stuff! And not just pizza. He gives us his land, his rivers, his air, his oxygen, his beaches, his puppies, his trees, his stones, his essential oils, his beef, his chicken, his veggies, his grapes, his grain, his hops, our bodies, our minds, our kids, our friends, technology, everything. It's all God's, but God loves to share. "Enjoy it!" he laughs. "Enjoy my stuff! Have a slice or two! Or six! I love you and want to share this with you."

But God has one request—that we share it with others, that we use "some" of these blessings to bless others. This is the "rent" he wants to collect, the love he wants us to give. If you like fancy church words, we call this *stewardship*. That means God is the owner and we are the stewards, or the managers, who care for his stuff in a way that makes him happy.

Need more examples? How about our words? God gives each of us a mouth and teeth and a tongue that produce tens of thousands of words each day, and he wants some of those words to build up others, to encourage them, to apologize to them, to make them happy to work at this job or go to this church. That's the rent.

Or how about the time that God gives us? Week after week he gives us 168 hours, and he wants some of those hours every week to be spent on spiritual community, on gathering together, in doing life together, on mutual confession and praying and forgiving and loving the least of these. That's the rent.

If all that weren't enough, God gives us amazing

technology—emails and texts and posts, and he wants some of that tech time to be about others. What can I give to these people? How can I bless them? How can I show them a glimpse of God's love? And the rent isn't optional (rent never is). It's required.

But here is where our story gets tricky, because God has "moved away." He's not physically here in flesh and blood. Which means there are not immediate consequences to our attitudes and actions as renters. But if we don't pay the rent, God will send a servant to collect, to correct. Your parents. Your teachers. Your fellow Christians. Maybe even your critics. And those are the moments when we learn if we're smart or, to quote God, stupid.

When those moments come, when someone finds the courage to confront you, I hope you avoid five very stupid reactions. Here they are:

1—Ignore. Ignore the correction. Say, "Whatever!" and delete the email, ignore the advice, act like the conversation never happened. Don't pray about it or take it to heart.

2—Excuse. Excuse your sin. "Maybe I don't care about her needs because she doesn't care about mine." "I pushed my brother because he pushed me first." "I was having a bad day, okay?" "I've been dealing with a lot, okay?" "Well, did you hear what she said about me?"

3—Defend. Defend your badness with your own

goodness. "Well, if I'm such a bad wife, why do I go to work and pick up the kids and cook for you? Huh?" "If my work is so bad, what about this project and this compliment and all the people who appreciate what I do?" It's when you list as many good works as you can think of so the scales tip and make everyone forget about the actual point of the conversation.

4—Attack. Attack your correctors. "Oh, like you should talk. Like you've never messed up. Like you're so perfect. Remember when you . . . Okay, well then I have something to say too when we're done with this."

5—Avoid. Avoid them altogether. Find new friends. These friends don't really support you. Find a new church. This one is too judgmental. Don't reply to the email. Just run away with the "rent."

That is so tempting, but that would be stupid. Don't be stupid. Not only will you miss out on the chance to grow spiritually, but you will have to face the owner, the landlord, the judge. Jesus is coming back, and he will judge the living and the dead. Eternity is a terrible thing to waste for an extra piece of fruit.

ETERNITY IS A TERRIBLE THING TO WASTE.

I got emotional reading Jesus' story. Angry, actually. I was angry at the wretched renters but also at the owner. These deadbeats beat his servants, smacked them around, killed them; then the owner sent his son? I got mad as I read. Why would he do that? That is so stupid. I wouldn't do that. Why would he do that?

But then it hit me. He did it because of me, because of you. God could have just come back and judged. But he didn't. He waited. He pleaded. He tried. He sent servant after servant. God loves us so much that even if he had to send his Son, he would try. That's not stupid. That's stupendous.

And maybe that's why you and I are here and Jesus is not. God could have fixed our pain yesterday. He could have ended cancer and war and abuse and death. Some people don't believe in God because he doesn't end pain and suffering. He could! He will on the Last Day. But then the pain and suffering of unbelievers would last forever. So he waits. He holds back despite his deep desire to dry our tears and end our suffering. The Bible says, "[God] **is patient with you, not wanting anyone to perish, but everyone to come to repentance**" (2 Peter 3:9). He doesn't want anyone to die clutching on to the rent, holding on to their sin. That's why you are reading this. God is reaching out to you, holding out his arms to you, sending another servant to remind you of his loving heart. So die to your defensiveness. Die to your claim to ownership. Declare your status as a renter, and you will find eternal life on the Father's land.

Your sin will not stop you from being saved. Your past will not stop you from being saved. Nothing you have done can trump the forgiveness of God's one and only Son. So give it to Jesus. He is right here on your doorstep, and there are nail marks in his hands, wounds from his cross, proof of his love for you. The cornerstone is right here, wanting you to be a living stone in this holy Christian church. This is what is marvelous in our eyes. That God would take the rejected stone, the Son put on a cross, and build his church upon it. That is not stupid. That is the smartest thing God ever did.

STUDY QUESTIONS

1. Which characteristics of God do you find in the parable of the tenants? What do these mean for you as a child of God?

2. What sinful characteristics did the tenants exhibit? Are you prone to exhibit any of the same things? What do you need to do to change?

3. On a scale of 1-10, how correctable do you think you are?

4. Challenge: Ask a friend, a relative, and a coworker to rate you on that same scale.

5. Name at least three reasons why having a teachable heart is essential to following Jesus.

CHAPTER 7

DON'T FORGET YOU ARE FORGIVEN

To get from where you are to where you want to be takes motivation. That's why mothers and marketers use rewards and threats and guilt and limited time offers and ice cream and 30 percent off coupons and a thousand other ways to motivate us to do what they want. They believe there is no movement without motivation.

That's also true with God. To get from where we are now to where God wants us to be takes motivation. And while God uses consequences and rewards and threats and blessings (read the book of Proverbs for proof of this), he relies on one primary thing to motivate us: his undeserved love.

If God had a motivation equation, it might be this: $M = R2$. Our motivation to serve God (M) is equal to our recognition of our sin times our recognition of

God's love (R2). If, like that sinful woman who poured perfume on Jesus' feet in Luke's gospel, we recognize how much we've sinned and how often God forgives us, we will be moved, compelled, and motivated to live for God.

In this chapter I want to tackle something that requires massive amounts of motivation: forgiveness. Look at the question one of Jesus' disciples asked: **"Then Peter came to Jesus and asked, 'Lord, how many times shall I forgive my brother or sister who sins against me? Up to seven times?'"** (Matthew 18:21). This is not some dry, academic, theological question, is it? When someone sins against you, it is visceral. It consumes your thoughts and squats down in your gut.

Even the memories of those sins can disturb us. Your spouse ignores her vows. She raises her voice, exaggerates ("You never think about me!"), brings up the past, rarely admits her wrongs, and cares so much about winning the fight and so little about your marriage. Your parents act like children. They get drunk like they're in college, get dramatic like they're going through puberty, and make you wish they wouldn't call, wouldn't stop by, wouldn't interfere. Your sister pursues her PhD in criticism. She always has an opinion about how you parent and where you work and how you spend your money. Then there's your ex, the one who tells everyone a very biased version of what ended your marriage.

And what do you do with the opposing team that

plays dirty every year? When they're throwing elbows at you (or at your kid) and whining when they don't get their way? And what do you do with classmates who make every morning a sickening moment? The ones who always have some joke, some comment, some whispering, some laughing at your expense? And what do you do with school administrators who seem too proud to listen or pessimistic coworkers who suck the joy out of every conversation or referees who are shamelessly biased or neighbors who care more about their lawn than they do about being neighborly? When someone sins against you, when the very thought of their face makes you feel sick, what are you supposed to do? How often do you forgive a serial sinner? Up to seven times? That's Peter's question. And it's personal for all of us.

Before we get our answer to that question from Jesus, let's remember what forgiveness means in the Bible. Forgiveness isn't minimizing sin ("it's not a big deal") or justifying sin ("you didn't know better") or reconciling a relationship **FORGIVENESS** ("I guess we're friends again") **IS THE OPPOSITE** or forgetting what happened ("forgive and forget"). For- **OF VENGEANCE.** giving someone doesn't mean there won't be consequences or tough conversations or even calling the police. No, in the Bible, forgiveness is the opposite of vengeance. It's putting aside that natural desire to pay another person back. It means refusing to hurt them for how they hurt you. Instead of trying to hurt them with your fists, with your words, with your cold shoulder, or with your next Facebook posts, you are going to forgive.

So how many times should we forgive? How many times do we refuse to get them back? **"Jesus answered, 'I tell you, not seven times, but seventy-seven times'"** (Matthew 18:22). Wait, what? 77 times? (Some translations think this means 70 times 7 times!) "Um, Jesus, sin hurts. It's hard to forgive one time, and you want 77 straight 'I forgive yous' (or 490?!)?" I think we're going to need a little help with this one. Scratch that—a lot of help. To get from what you and I do now to what Jesus wants us to do next time, we're going to need a lot of motivation.

That's why Jesus continued with a story: **"Therefore, the kingdom of heaven is like a king who wanted to settle accounts with his servants. As he began the settlement, a man who owed him ten thousand bags of gold was brought to him"** (Matthew 18:23,24). One day a king wants to balance the books, to settle every dime and dollar of his servants' debts. A guy comes who owes him 10,000 bags of gold. A single bag of gold was about 20 years' worth of salary. At $35,000/year, that's $700,000 for one bag! But this guy owes 10,000 bags of gold. That's 200,000 years' worth of salary! That's $7 billion! How in the world did this guy get $7 billion in the hole? Did he have a gambling problem? Did he bet the farm on the Milwaukee Brewers winning the World Series? We don't know, but we do know this guy is in deep trouble.

"Since he was not able to pay, the master ordered that he and his wife and his children and all that he had be sold to repay the debt. At this the servant fell on his knees before him. 'Be patient with me' he begged, 'and I will pay back everything'" (verses 25,26). Right . . . pay back 200,000 years' worth of wages? He was in too deep.

But check this out: **"The servant's master took pity on him, canceled the debt and let him go"** (verse 27). What? Why does the king take pity on him? Why does he have even an ounce of compassion? This isn't a guy who made a little mistake. This is a guy who owes big time. To be honest, I don't know why the king has pity, but Jesus says that's what the king does. He cancels the debt. No payment plan. No extension on the loan. Just $7 billion cancelled. "Go in peace, your debt is forgiven."

Sound crazy? Yeah. Sound familiar? It should. A person with an absurd debt he can't pay. A king with absurd compassion who forgives the entire amount. That sounds a bit like us and God.

I once read a story from another Christian author about a Russian czar who had a trusted general who was dying of his wounds. To repay him for his faithful service, the czar promised to raise the general's son as his own child. And that's exactly what he did. He gave the boy the best education in Russia and opportunities only royalty had. He gave him a generous commission and a coveted position in the Russian army. But the young man had a problem. Gambling. What started as something small and manageable grew into an animal he couldn't control. Not only did he spend all his money, but he began to "borrow" funds from his regiment, hoping to win big and pay them all back, of course. But he didn't win, and the borrowed funds grew and grew and grew. The young man was in deep, deeper than he ever imagined.

One night as he looked at the books, he realized he couldn't hide his sin anymore. His embezzlement would soon be discovered. He would bring shame to himself, his father, and the czar. So the young man found a bottle of cheap vodka and his pistol. He drank shot after shot, summoning the courage to take another kind of shot. But the drinks were too strong, and he passed out on the books before he got around to pulling the trigger.

That same night, however, the czar was doing what he often did. In disguise, he walked among his troops, eavesdropping on their conversations. Curious, he peeked into his foster son's tent and saw him slumped over a book, vodka and bullets nearby. The czar crept over, read the book, and realized what his son had done and what he was about to do.

Hours later, the young man's throbbing hangover woke him up. But when he looked around, his gun was gone. In its place there was a note. His fuzzy eyes tried to focus on the handwriting, which seemed familiar. It read, "I, the czar, will pay the full amount from my personal funds to account for the debt in this book." On the bottom was the fresh red ink of the czar's personal seal. His "father" had seen his sin clearly and paid for it personally.

That is just like our story with the Father. We have a debt to God we cannot pay. What started as a little sin only grew as we got older until the very quantity of our sin was absurd. At just 100 sins/day, if you are 40, you have already committed 1.46 million sins. Like the gambling young man and the 10,000 bags of gold servant, you and I can't pay this back. No one can. And every day doesn't decrease our debt but only adds to our sin.

WE HAVE A DEBT TO GOD WE CANNOT PAY.

But God paid it. He came into this world, he walked among us, he saw how bad our sin was, and he died to pay for all of it. Jesus' blood, shed on a cross, was God's official seal of payment. Why did he do it? I honestly don't know. He canceled the debt. Why would he do it? I can't logically make sense of it. At the cross, Jesus shouted, "It is finished! Paid in full!" and he settled the account. No payment plan, no loan extension, no probationary period. Jesus just forgave, not 7 times, not 77 times, but 7 billion times. Our billion-dollar spiritual debt has been forgiven. So go in peace; your sins are forgiven.

Actually, don't go just yet. Because Jesus' story doesn't end there. **"But when that servant went out, he found one of his fellow servants who owed him a hundred silver coins."** (That's 100 days' wages. Maybe $15,000. A real debt.) **"He grabbed him and began to choke him. 'Pay back what you owe me!' he** demanded. His fellow servant fell to his knees and begged him, 'Be patient with me, and I will pay it back.' But he refused. Instead, he went off and had the man thrown into prison until he could pay the debt" (Matthew 18:28-30). Things get ugly. He wraps his fingers around the debtor's throat and pushes him against a wall. His eyes bulge. The servant catches his breath; the debtor begs for a little time, a little compassion, but the servant refuses. There is no pity, no compassion, no forgiveness. After all, a debt is a debt. The man owes him. Makes you gag, doesn't it?

Don't gag too soon, because I bet someone owes you. There are debts right here in our hearts as real as last week. Someone owes you. Sin robs us of happiness and joy and peace, so those who sin against us have robbed us; they owe us; they have a debt to us. They owe us our childhood back, our senior year, a happy marriage, a school where our kids don't come home crying. It feels like someone has to pay.

And sometimes we decide to make them pay. Does it ever get ugly, like fingers wrapped around a throat? You come right back at your wife with a more creative insult, with a pounding fist, with a name no man should call his wife. You run to Facebook to post your payback for 232 friends to read, 232 allies against that idiot who hurt you. You come home and vent about your boss again, choking his reputation to death with your stories of his sins. You wait until the ref is out of earshot for your trash talk. You shout your opinion about the officials for the entire gym to hear. You text back while the rage clouds your judgment and leave the caps lock on. You withhold sex because you know it will kill him. Or maybe your ugly payback is not doing anything at all. You don't say anything good about him, even when he deserves it. You don't work hard when she's not looking. You don't call or invite or love or do anything. When you choose payback instead of forgiveness, it's always ugly.

"When the other servants saw what had happened, they were outraged and went and told their master everything that had happened. Then the master called the servant in. 'You wicked servant,' he said, 'I canceled all that debt of yours because you begged me to. Shouldn't you have had mercy on your fellow servant just as I had on you?'" (Matthew 18:31-33). "How could you? Did you forget what I did? Didn't you have every reason to have mercy, to show pity, to forgive, just as I forgave you?" **"In anger his master handed him over to the jailers to be tortured, until he should pay back all he owed. This is how my heavenly Father will treat each of you unless you forgive your brother or sister from your heart"** (verses 34,35).

There's no warm, fuzzy, comfortable ending to Jesus' story. Just a shocking lesson on forgiveness. The point? Jesus says it is scandalously wrong for the forgiven not to forgive. In fact, Jesus insists there is no such thing as a Christian who insists on payback. Let me put that down here again: There is no such thing as a Christian who insists on payback. Let me clarify: There are plenty of people who live for payback, who live with a spirit of revenge, but they are not true Christians. And there are billions of Christians who struggle with payback, who hurt those who hurt them and hate the reaction. I am one of them. Every Christian is one of them, because we struggle with doing what's right. But there is no such thing as a Christian who insists on payback, who insists on settling accounts, who refuses the idea of forgiveness. Because how can you claim to be part of a religion of forgiveness and yet insist on not forgiving?

Jesus' point, his motivation for our forgiveness is this: Don't forget you're forgiven. Because if you forget you're forgiven, you'll forget to forgive. If you forget the $7 billion you've been forgiven, you'll forget to forgive the $15,000 you're owed.

That's what happened with Sarah. Sarah and I never really got along. She loved church traditions; I loved trying new things. Neither one of us was right. But things went wrong. She got mad and let me know it. Snide comments just before the church service started. Crossed arms and rolled eyes as I was trying to lead worship. A long, critical letter with a few below-the-belt shots. Looking back, I can see why she was so mad. I was changing what she loved so much about our church. But she did sin against me, more than seven times. And I didn't take it well. I tried to smile, but inside the thoughts were ugly. I didn't love her like a pastor should, like a Christian should.

That's why I invited her to talk. It was awkward, but I tried to listen to how I could improve our relationship and, at the same time, I shared with her how I felt. "I don't feel loved by you, respected by you." And do you know what she said? I'll never forget it. Sarah said, "I know. I'm trying."

That's when it hit me. I know someone exactly like that, someone who knows what he should do and tries and fails, someone whose progress with Christian love isn't so obvious most days. That's me. I do that. I'm just like her. But God keeps forgiving me, so how can I not keep forgiving her? I was so focused on her sin that I forgot about my forgiveness. And when you forget you're forgiven, you forget to forgive.

Remember the motivation equation? $M = R2$. Your motivation to forgive is based on two things: Your recognition of your own sin and your recognition of God's merciful, billion-dollar-debt-canceling love. If you don't forget those two things, forgiveness will not be easy, but it will be your desire. You will not justify your payback. You will want what God wants: to forgive them as he has forgiven you.

I've never met someone sinned against so horribly like Natalie. I met her at the Pizza Ranch (where all good stories begin . . .). Spotting the curious tattoo behind her ear, I started a conversation, which led to a meeting at church, which led to the most horrific story I've ever heard. As a child living in Australia, she was abused, molested, and violated by those who shared her last name. She ran away from home, angry at God, searching for anything to medicate her pain and ended up at a homeless shelter. There Natalie met a young man who said he had a place to stay and invited her to crash with him for a bit. She agreed, went to his place, had a drink, passed out, and woke up in a nightmare. Chained to a bed in his garage, Natalie became part of the stories that are too traumatic to process. For days, weeks, months, she was enslaved as her "friend" made money selling her body to anyone with enough cash. The story would only get worse before getting better. Before escaping her slavery and making it to America, Natalie would be betrayed by a social worker, enslaved and sold for another three years, and literally stabbed in the back, barely escaping murder. By God's grace, she is now safe and has come to believe in the miraculous grace of God. The tattoo I saw that day at the Pizza Ranch reads, "Not for Sale," with a small cross beneath it.

While I'll never forget Natalie's story, what struck me most was not the sin of those men but the spirit of that woman. "I forgive them," Natalie insisted. "I pray for them that they would find God like I did."

"How?" I wondered, trying to imagine not hating such monsters. Her answer was simple:

"Because God forgave me. During my life, I rebelled against God, hated him, sinned against him, but he forgave me. He forgave all of me. That's why I forgive them." Natalie knows what Jesus did. She's trying to forgive them too.

Where do you find the motivation to forgive not 7 times but 77 times? Don't forget you're forgiven, and you won't forget to forgive.

STUDY QUESTIONS

1. Think about those who have hurt you most in your life. How have you treated them in return? If necessary, bring your "payback" to God in confession.

2. Read Matthew 5:43-48. Brainstorm two to three things you could do to bless the people you thought about in the question above. Then craft a plan to put these things into action as you imitate your forgiving Father in heaven.

3. Why do you think the devil loves to keep you remembering someone else's wrong?

4. Read Ephesians 4:29-32. What do these verses have to do with the parable of the unmerciful servant and this book chapter?

5. Write a prayer thanking God for his mercy and forgiveness.

CHAPTER 8
GO DOWN TO GO UP

What do you think would happen if a ringless teenager with a six-month baby bump showed up at your church? What would you do (or not do)? What would you say (or not say)? How would she feel? While you're thinking about that, what would someone experience at your small group Bible study if they confessed a messy history—a sexual sin or even a sexual crime? If they were a RSO (registered sex offender), in NA (narcotics anonymous), or had a PO (parole officer), what would be your MO (modus operandi or "way of operating")? Those questions force us to think about the kind of people we are and what kind of people we would like to be.

Jesus tells us the best place to start answering those complicated questions. He does so through a story, one of the most preposterous, ridiculous, surprising, and beautiful stories Jesus ever told.

"To some who were confident of their own

righteousness and looked down on everybody else, Jesus told this parable: 'Two men went up to the temple to pray, one a Pharisee and the other a tax collector'" (Luke 18:9,10). Jesus could not have chosen two more different men for the lead parts in his story. Pharisees were first-century "good guys." The name Pharisee actually comes from a word that means "set apart," which is exactly what they were. The Pharisees were set apart from the spiritually lukewarm majority of humanity. They were passionate about God, devoted to the church, committed to prayer, dedicated to giving, staunch about the Bible, and fanatical about faith. When a Pharisee looked into the mirror, he said, "Fair, I see," because his life was fair and beautiful compared to the average man (get it?).

"And the other a tax collector." Cue the change in soundtrack. The tax collectors were first-century villains. We may not adore IRS auditors, but the Israelites hated tax collectors. When the Roman Empire took over Israel, they allowed the locals to bid for tax-collecting purposes. The winning bid would become a tax collector and was given legal authority to charge whatever he wanted and even given Roman muscle to ensure everybody paid up. Tax collectors got stinking rich while driving their own people into stinking poverty. Imagine a Polish man offering the Nazis the whereabouts of his fellow Jews for a few bucks, and you'll understand how people felt about tax collectors.

These were two radically different men, and they lived two radically different lifestyles. **"The Pharisee** stood up by himself and prayed: 'God, I thank you that I am not like other people—robbers, evildoers, adulterers—or even like this tax collector. I fast twice a week and give a tenth of all I get'" (Luke 18:11,12). Exactly what we'd expect from a "fair" Pharisee. No ripping off people by force. No ripping apart marriages by flirtation gone too far. No ripping up the nation by siding with the Romans. Pharisees were much better than that. This one fasted twice a week. The Old Testament commanded Jews to take one day every year off of eating, the Day of Atonement. But this Pharisee was better than that, 104 times better! Every Monday and every Thursday, let's say, 104 days every year, the Pharisee wouldn't touch food! (And I'm impressed if I skip second dinner to do a home devotion.) He gave a tenth of all he got. No leftovers when the offering plate came around. No giving after taxes. Ten percent right off the top. His lifestyle was as "set apart" as the name Pharisee suggested.

"But the tax collector stood at a distance. He would not even look up to heaven, but beat his breast" (verse 13). Exactly what we'd expect from a tax collector. What was he supposed to say in front of God? While the Pharisee was fasting on Monday, he was forcing his neighbors to hand over their lunch money. While the Pharisee's stomach was groaning on Thursday, he was making widows groan over their emptied pockets. While the Pharisee was giving 10 percent to God, he was extorting 30 percent from the people of God. There was nothing fair, nothing beautiful about the tax collector's life . . . and he knew it. He couldn't even come close to God, couldn't even look up to God, couldn't do anything but pound his pitiful chest, which contained his pitiful heart.

Two radically different men. Two radically different lifestyles. And two radically different prayers. **"The Pharisee . . . prayed, 'God, I thank you that I am not like other people.'"** "God, I know you accept me because I am acceptable. Look what I'm bringing to you. Look what I've done that they haven't. Look what I resisted that they didn't. Look how I've improved, how I've served, how I've devoted myself. I'm fair, you see." **"But the tax collector . . . said, 'God, have mercy on me, a sinner.'"** "God, accept an unacceptable man like me. I have nothing to bring to you. I haven't done what he has. I did what he didn't. I haven't improved, haven't served, haven't been devoted. I'm a sinner, I see. So have mercy on me."

Two radically different prayers and, according to Jesus, two radically different results. He concludes, **"I tell you that this man** [the tax collector], **rather than the other, went home justified before God. For all those who exalt themselves will be humbled, and those who humble themselves will be exalted"** (Luke 18:14). Surprise! The self-proclaimed good guy ends up guilty. The self-proclaimed sinner ends up saved. The one who morally exalts himself ends up humbled while the morally humble ends up exalted.

One of London's highest places can only be reached by going down. St. Paul's Cathedral is an architectural giant in England, towering over downtown London. One of the most stunning views is located just at the base of the massive dome, 637 steps up. But to reach the apex of the dome, the highest point, where a massive golden cross stands, one has to enter through a small door and first descend a few steps. That door displays a small sign that reads: "Go down to go up." Sound familiar? **"Those who humble themselves will be exalted."**

So let me ask the question that Jesus kept forcing his audience to answer—Which of the two is most like you? Where does your fairness, your righteousness, come from? How do you approach God in prayer? The start of Jesus' story makes us probe into our hearts—**"To some who were confident of their own righteousness and looked down on everyone else, Jesus told this parable"** (verse 9).

The litmus test for self-righteousness is how you compare yourself to everybody else. "God, I've done a lot of good in my life. I took care of my sick parents unlike my brother, I volunteered at my church unlike the folks who only come on Sunday, and I gave to charity unlike my boss. Compared to most, I'm a pretty good person. God, I haven't done anything terribly bad. I've never murdered like those terrorists or committed adultery like my ex-boyfriend or stolen from work like the guy from accounting. God, I take you seriously enough to pray every day and come to church more than just on Christmas and Easter like those nominal Christians. God, I work hard and don't drain the system like 'those' people. I got my degree. I get up for work. I didn't have three kids with three women. God, I keep my promises unlike those politicians. I care about the future of our country unlike those freeloaders. God, I thank you that I am not like other men. I know that you accept me because of what I've done. I know you'll save me because of how I've tried. I know you'll be good to me because I've been good . . . not like those people." But **"those who exalt themselves will be humbled."**

HUMBLE YOURSELF NOW TO BE EXALTED LATER.

There's a better prayer, a better way, a better result. Go down to go up. Humble yourself now to be exalted later. Speak those two words—*I confess.* "God, I haven't done enough good in my life. I took care of my sick parents, but my heart was often uncompassionate. I volunteered at church to impress them, not because I was impressed by you. I've never murdered, but I've hated. I've never cheated, but I've fantasized. I've never robbed, but I've wasted time at work. God, I pray to you, but mostly for me and not for them, mostly for earthly stuff instead of spiritual strength. God, I come to church, but I miss most of the point and can barely focus through a single prayer. God, I've judged those people instead of praying for them, avoided those people instead of loving them, expected those people to act more Christian instead of telling them about Christ. God, I am just like other men. In fact, if I'm counting, I'm worse than other men. You shouldn't accept me because of what I've done. You shouldn't save me because I haven't tried hard enough. You shouldn't be good to me because I'm not good, not as good as you demand. I'm not fair, I see. So have mercy on me." **"Those who humble themselves will be exalted."**

Can I tell you something beautiful? Jesus loved tax collectors. Nearly every time they appear in the Bible, Jesus is choosing them, calling them, eating with them, forgiving them, saving them, changing them, and telling the shocked crowds that they are entering the kingdom of God. Can I tell you something even more beautiful? Jesus hasn't changed. We come to Jesus like tax collectors with only a humble confession, and Jesus exalts us! Jesus gives us his righteousness. Jesus' face beams, and he calls us his friends. He wants to sit and eat with us and tell us of our exaltation and inspire us to live new and holy lives. Jesus lifts us up from our confession and says such exalted things: "You **JESUS EXALTS US!** are forgiven. God loves you. I have made you good, better, the best you could be. You believe in me, and that means you are what I am— holy, righteous, perfect, pure. You are fair, you see; not because of you, but because of me!"

God is fair, you see, fairer and more beautiful than we can ever fathom. Jesus, the Son of God, came into this world and humbled himself to serve us, to love us, to live a fair and holy life for us, to die on a cross for us. He was humiliated for our sin so we could be exalted.

Jesus is the one who justifies us, declares us not guilty before God. Jesus is the one who purifies us, wiping away all the evidence of sin. Jesus is the one who reconciles us, ending the righteous anger God had over our unrighteousness. And that's all free! It's all grace! It's for all!

So what would a prostitute and a felon and an addict and a single mom and a divorced dad think if they came to a church like yours and mine? I hope they would find people willing to slide over and make room for another sinner, just like us, so they could hear about Jesus and be exalted just like us. I hope they would come to see their sin as wretchedly as we see ours and see their Savior as clearly as we see him.

My prayer is that we would become the kind of people who go up by going down. I pray honest confession would be a virtue and not a vice. I pray tax collectors and teachers and prostitutes and pastors would worship together, all confessing their sin and all finding righteousness in Jesus alone. I pray our small groups would not be superficial studies but be filled with real struggles and real reminders that there is grace even for that. I pray first-time "sinners" would be surprised that long-time "saints" confess so quickly and so honestly. I pray our classrooms would be safe havens for confession instead of self-righteous competitions. I pray you would be afraid of missing out on the exalted blessings that only come through confessing the truth, the whole truth, and nothing but the truth. I pray we would hate the sins of our culture, but no more than we hate our own, of which we are immensely more familiar. I pray we would celebrate the great work of God that is on display every time someone says, "I confess."

God, make us and keep us that kind of people!

STUDY QUESTIONS

1. Do you think Pharisees get an unfair reputation in our day given their passion for the Bible and their desire not to conform to the sins of their culture? Who today is most like the Pharisees (very religious, very devout, very tempted to think they are better than others)?

2. Karma is the belief that you have to do good works in order to outweigh your sins. How does this story prove that Jesus didn't believe in karma?

3. Agree/Disagree: Christianity makes forgiveness too easy.

4. Read Romans 3:19-26, one of the Bible's best sections on how to be righteous (right with God). Find at least three phrases that prove that we are righteous through Jesus and not through our good works.

5. Can you think of anyone who would benefit from this short story from Jesus? Who? And what made you think of them? After answering these questions, pray for the right words and reach out to share this message.

CHAPTER 9

CHANGE YOUR MIND AND THEN BELIEVE

I recognized Mark as soon as I saw him zipping down the sidewalk. The overstuffed backpack that he and other homeless men lug around town. The energetic eyes I had noticed when he showed up at church the previous Sunday. Mark must have recognized me too because he immediately decided to take our second-ever conversation in a spiritual direction.

"I'm going to hell," he declared.

"Why do you think that?" I responded.

"Because I'm selfish," he said.

"Me too," I confessed. "I'd love to talk about that sometime."

Mark shook my hand and continued on his way, convinced he was still on his way to hell.

I actually meet a lot of people like Mark. They jump from a truth (I'm a sinner) to an assumption (I must be going to hell). And since they can't undo their sin, they go through life thinking they have no hope of eternal life. The SS *Better Place* has sailed, and they didn't have the moral resources to buy a ticket. It's too late, and there's nothing to be done about it.

Some people are pretty brash about it. "The church would burn down if I stepped in!" they joke. (I wonder if the joking is a defense mechanism to cope with the fear of it all?) After all the shot taking, pot smoking, commandment breaking, rule bending, church skipping, prayer missing, people using, and people abusing, they conclude that God would instantly combust any congregation that dared to open their doors to 21st-century tax collectors like them. Maybe others have earned a seat in the "house of God," but not them. It's too late.

Have you ever thought that? As you look back on your past, are you pretty sure that you have messed up one too many times? Perhaps you see the damage that addiction has done to your body, that your anger has done to your family, that your infidelity has done to your ex, that your worry has done to your faith, and you jump to the assumption that the damage must be spiritual too. The gap between you and God is too big. It's simply too late.

Or maybe you rarely, if ever, think that. Maybe your tendency is not to see the moral difference between you and God but the massive difference between you and them. You are—and this is just being honest—different. Different than the monster whose confiscated computer

106

was filled with images of underage children. Different than the insatiable CEOs who gorge themselves on more millions even as their employees struggle to pay for groceries. Different than all the people who look like they're not even trying to be good. You haven't lived a perfect life, but you have tried your best to learn from your mistakes, to mature in your faith, and to do the right thing as often as you can. When the headlines are filled with unthinkable evil, our natural conclusion is that we are better and bound for a better place.

I know there are plenty of variations on those two beliefs, but I wonder if you and the people you love either think you're obviously going to hell or you're obviously going to heaven. I bet a bunch.

Years ago, a grad school professor told me the fastest way to figure out a person's faith is to ask them two questions: First, if you died today, how sure are you that you would go to heaven? Second, why did you answer the way you did? Those questions cut to the heart of what we believe about who is in, who is out, and how we can tell the difference between the two.

But our assumptions about eternity aren't anything new. A massive percentage of the people whom Jesus met in the 1st century thought the same things that we think in the 21st century. The tax collectors and prostitutes assumed it was too late. There was no chance. They had fallen too far. The Pharisees and religious leaders saw the obvious difference between their behavior and "those people's" and assumed, naturally, that they were "in."

That's why Jesus told a story about two sons. Matthew, a former tax collector, who was there to hear it, wrote it down so that we could learn from it. Let's study this little chunk of Matthew chapter 21.

"What do you think? There was a man who had two sons. He went to the first and said, 'Son, go and work today in the vineyard'" (Matthew 21:28). This parable is about a dad who had two sons and some yard work to be done. Simple enough. But notice a few key points in Jesus' carefully chosen words:

Go—There is a command here. Not a suggestion ("It would be nice if you would consider . . ."). Not an opinion ("I think today would be a great day to . . ."). Not a polite request ("If you can find the time . . ."). No, this is an order. A demand. A command. "Go! Get up! Get the job done!"

Work—There is sweat here. Work implies effort, exertion, and energy spent. This isn't typing up a few emails in an air-conditioned office but digging in the soil under the throbbing heat of the Middle Eastern sun. This is how you feel about pulling weeds in your overgrown yard or shoveling seven inches of wet snow.

Today—There is urgency here. This father isn't giving his son the freedom to choose which day he prefers to do the work but instead demanding the work be done now. "Scrap your plans, kid, because your dad has made a demand."

Put all those words together and what do you get? A triple whammy against human autonomy. These are hard words to hear even when spoken by a loving father to his beloved son. I dare you to go up to someone you love and order them to do something *now.* Interrupt their scheduled plans and command them (not suggest/ ask) to do hard work that might take them all day to finish. Their gut reaction will help you appreciate the next part of Jesus' story. **"'I will not'** [the first son] **answered"** (verse 29). "No, Dad, I don't want to. I won't." While I don't think the kid is right, I can relate to his reaction. Even as a grown-up, I like my plans, my schedule, and my comfort. "Would you please help me?" is an interruption that I might consider, but "Do this now!" is a demand that would bring out my inner rebel.

"But later he changed his mind and went" (verse 29). *But later.* Those two words are essential to Jesus' story, so highlight them here and stick them in the back of your brain. This son started off on the wrong foot *but later* changed his mind about his rebellious ways. His initial answer must have disappointed his father, *but later* his behavior brought a smile to his dad's face.

What changed? While Jesus doesn't give us the details of this son's thought process, something must have been powerful enough to overcome his reluctance. Did he think about the love of his father and all the sacrifices that the father had made for him over the years? Did he think about how uncomfortable dinner would be if he doubled down on his "I will not"? Did his conscience gnaw at him, making his soft bed more uncomfortable than the stiff soil of the vineyard? We aren't sure, but we do know that something changed. He eventually obeyed. To use a New Testament term, he *repented*.

But Jesus' story isn't over. **"Then the father went to the other son and said the same thing. He answered, 'I will, sir'"** (verse 30). Same father, same request. "Go. Work. Today." But this time the answer is impressively obedient. Don't miss the details.

I—In Jesus' original Greek, this little word is emphatic. Picture the second son laying a sincere hand over his heart and pausing after the *I*, emphasizing the difference between his desire to honor his father and his brother's self-serving heart. He is pointing out the contrast, the superiority of his morality.

Will—There is desire here. "I want to, Father. I plan to, Dad." This is a step beyond obedience. This is service with a smile.

Sir—What respect! Most parents would accept a grumbling, "Fine," as long as the work got done. But this son honors his father, acknowledges his authority, and promises to get the job done. This son is about to be the poster boy for the commandment to honor your father and your mother.

Except he didn't. Jesus says, **"He answered, 'I will, sir,' but he did not go"** (verse 30). This promising son didn't get to the finish line. In fact, he barely started the race. Why? What happened? Jesus doesn't say, but we can imagine the son staring at the

HE LOOKED SO GOOD, BUT HE FELL FAR SHORT.

sun, realizing how much work this project would be. In the end, he didn't do anything. He looked so good, but he fell far short of his father's orders.

Jesus asked, **"Which of the two did what his father wanted?"** (verse 31). I shared our Savior's question with my oldest daughter. I told her Jesus' story of the two sons and asked her which one of them obeyed his loving father. She paused, "Neither!" I laughed (and agreed). Then I said, "Neither son was perfect in his response. But—what do you think?—if you had to choose between the two, which of the sons would you rather have?" Brooklyn said, "The first one." I smiled and agreed (again). As a father, I would rather have a stubborn kid who comes around than one who, upon further thought, doesn't think obeying me is worth it.

The religious leaders of Jesus' day thought the same thing. **"'Which of the two did what his father wanted?' 'The first,' they answered'"** (verse 31). Better late than never. Better to change your mind about your original sin than to decide, upon further thought, that your father isn't worth it in the end.

But then Jesus transitioned from his made-up story to a real-life application. I wish I could have seen the Pharisees' faces when Jesus dropped this atomic bomb: **"Truly I tell you, the tax collectors and the prostitutes are entering the kingdom of God ahead of you"** (verse 31). The people everyone assumed were going to hell (the tax collectors and prostitutes) were getting into God's kingdom while the people everyone assumed were going to heaven (the Pharisees and religious leaders) were not.

Think for a moment how you would feel about these words if you had lived in those days. Imagine if Matthew the tax collector was your next-door neighbor. As you scrape together enough flour for a meager dinner, his servants bring home heaping portions of meat and the freshest of fruits. You prepare a feast, but Matthew has raised your taxes (again), forcing you to work extra hours just to get by. In your daydreams, you slam the door in his face, but you don't dare to do so in real life, not with Roman soldiers ready to enforce his greedy demands. Tax collectors are monsters. Sellouts. Me-first men who make a mess of Israel.

Prostitutes weren't much better. Some were victims of sex trafficking, captured during war and forced to make money for their masters in humiliating ways. Others, like Tamar in Genesis chapter 38, chose prostitution as a way to make full-time wages with part-time hours. The "oldest profession" was based off the simple economics of supply and demand. Many people wanted more sex (demand) than they could get (supply), and prostitutes took advantage of the gap.

But imagine if that profession intersected with your personal life. Imagine if your fiancé or father or mother or best friend's husband had a favorite prostitute. Imagine the relational wreckage when he walked through the door, smelling of her perfume. Picture your mother's face. See your sister-in-law rush to her room to hide her tears. Imagine the insecurity over the shape of your body or the anger you'd feel when your path crossed hers. Prostitutes made money off of such pain.

Jesus feels that pain too. These life-degrading sinners were as rebellious as the first son in Jesus' story. God had said, "You shall not steal. Give to the poor." But the tax collectors crossed their arms and said, "We won't. We don't want to." Our Father commanded, "You shall not commit adultery. Love your neighbor as yourself." But the prostitutes winked at their repeat customers and said, "We won't. We don't want to."

But later. Jesus' two-word phrase tells us that something changed in their heads and in their hearts, something so big that it changed what they did with their hands and their lives. This change was so immense that Jesus dared to say that the tax collectors and prostitutes were "entering the kingdom of God."

How?! I know we shouldn't demand anything of God's Son, but given the damage that the tax collectors and prostitutes caused, how can God just let them through the gates into the kingdom?

Jesus must have anticipated that reaction, but he explained, **"For John came to you to show you the way of righteousness, and you did not believe him, but the tax collectors and the prostitutes did"** (verse 32). How did it happen? Because these black sheep of Israel believed in John the Baptist's "way."

This is the most important phrase of the text, so let's slow down and make sure we get it—What exactly is the way of righteousness? It's the way to be "right" with God. Most people assume the way to be right with

God is to do enough right things and avoid enough wrong things. In their minds, the kingdom of God is like a palace down the street, and every good work gets you one step closer. This is why the Pharisees assumed they were basically at the gates and the prostitutes were ten miles back down the road.

But John the Baptist knew better. John knew that God is GOD—holy, perfect, flawless, righteous. God is so morally up there that he is unreachable for people down here. He is less like the palace down the road and more like the clouds up in the sky. Sure, you may be further down the road than me, but we are both approximately as far from the clouds as each other.

So if doing the right thing isn't "the way" to be right with God, what is? Go back to the early chapters of the gospels, study John's message, and you'll find two essential parts to this "way"—Repent and believe. Repent of your sins. You've been saying, "I won't!" to our Father. Change your mind. Stop playing God. Stop trying to tell the Lord what's right and wrong. Surrender and say, "Your will be done." And then believe. Believe in Jesus, the Lamb of God who takes away the sins of the world. John preached to everyone, to prostitutes and priests, to tax collectors and teachers of the law: "Repent and believe in Jesus, and you will be right with God. He is the only Way."

By the way, this is what the kingdom of God is all about. A kingdom is a place with a king, with someone who (1) rules with authority and (2) offers you safety. In God's kingdom, you don't get to be the king. You must acknowledge his authority. You must surrender your autonomy. You must—to use Jesus' phrase—change your mind. But don't be afraid to do so! God is the kind of King who is kind, a ruler who freely offers you

IN GOD'S KINGDOM, YOU ARE SAFE.

eternal safety. The walls of his forgiveness keep your sin, your shame, even hell itself far from you. In God's kingdom, you are safe now and will be forever.

Let's put all this together so Jesus' teaching makes sense. How do those two sons fit together with tax collectors, prostitutes, religious leaders, and John the Baptist? Here's how—The tax collectors and prostitutes were like the first son. At first, they didn't do what God wanted them to do. They played by their own rules. They insisted on getting the last word. They stole from and slept with their neighbors. But then John the Baptist came and, by the work of the Holy Spirit, they believed him! They "changed their minds" by repenting of their sins and looking to Jesus for their forgiveness. Read Matthew chapter 3 and Luke chapter 3 and see how Israel's worst sinners came to the Jordan River all wrong and, having believed John, left right with God.

The religious leaders, however, did not. Like the second son in Jesus' story, they seemed as righteous as people could be. "I will, Lord!" they said when God's Law was read in the synagogue. But they didn't. John told them to repent, but they didn't. John urged them to look to Jesus, but they didn't. And why not? Because they didn't think they needed to be saved. They were different than the tax collectors and prostitutes. They were better.

The end of Jesus' story brings us to the big question—Which of the two is most like you? As you think about the two sons, which of the two are you? I would love to say, "Neither!" but that wouldn't be true. My nature is too naughty for "neither." Yours is too.

Maybe, like Mark outside of my church, you are all too aware of your sins. You don't have to think hard to remember the "I won't!" you shouted at God as you did life your way. Maybe those choices came with consequences—a strained relationship with your parents, burned bridges with your siblings, a failed marriage, an abortion, a now-addicted brain, a sexually transmitted infection, a decade wasted on living essentially for yourself.

If that's you, there's still hope. Jesus said about a "son" like you, **"But later he changed his mind"** (Matthew 21:29). What does that mean? That even the worst of sinners can end up **"entering the kingdom of God"** (Matthew 21:31). Through repentance and faith in Jesus, you too can be saved.

This makes me think of my brothers in Christ who are behind bars. In one of my desk drawers, I keep a stack of letters that have been checked and stamped by the Wisconsin prison system. Since *Time of Grace* is broadcast in many prisons throughout my home state, many inmates hear me preach the "way of righteousness," and some of them are moved to tell me their stories. A theme I have noticed in their letters is living like the first son. For years these men did their own thing—drinking, using, hustling, threatening, controlling, clicking, stealing, sinning—habits that eventually backfired on them as sin always does. I read their heartbreaking stories of the people they hurt (or killed or trafficked), of the reputations that will never be restored in this life, of the freedom that is years away. But then they tell me about God's grace. Through prison chaplains, Christian "cellies" (the guy who shares your cell), and Christ-centered TV programs, they found a message that changed their minds. They repented of their rebelliousness and looked to Jesus for their forgiveness. Some law-abiding folks might not believe it, but those lawbreakers will make it into the kingdom of God, into a place where their souls will be safe for ever and ever. Like the first son, they experienced a "but later" moment.

THERE STILL IS A WAY FOR YOU TO BE RIGHT WITH GOD.

You can too. Maybe you thought your chances with God were long gone, but there still is a way for you to be right with God. His name is Jesus, and he is **"the way"** (John 14:6). He is a gracious King who has left the gates of his kingdom open to the least likely people. Yes, they are still open for you. Just ask the tax collectors and prostitutes.

That's true for "second sons" too. Perhaps your story is less of the black sheep variety and more like the Pharisees of Jesus' day. "Yes, Lord!" you said.

"Your will be done!" you prayed. But then you didn't do it. Compared to some of your family, you look good, but heaven isn't about how you compare to them but rather how you compare to him. Maybe you have never considered that possibility until this moment.

If so, I need to share the final line from this section of Matthew's gospel: **"Jesus said to them . . . 'And even after you saw this, you did not repent and believe him'"** (21:32). In a way, these are chilling words. The Pharisees went from stubborn to stubborner, refusing to follow the lead of the sinners who listened to John. Yet there is something else here too—Jesus' longing to save them still. No, the religious leaders didn't listen to John. They walked away dry while the tax collectors got wet in the baptismal waters of the Jordan River. Yet Jesus still reached out to them. He spoke in their synagogues, ate at their houses, answered their questions. Despite their disobedience to the Father, Jesus kept trying, kept preaching, kept praying for those who didn't know what they were doing. Matthew chapter 21 happened during Holy Week, which means that Jesus was still trying, still reaching out to those who refused to repent for three straight years. He still wanted them in the kingdom.

Early in my ministry, I met one of the nicest guys. He was an accomplished collegiate athlete, amazing husband, active father, successful businessman, and all-around nice guy. Someone invited him to our church and, soon after, he took the class to become an official member in our church family. During the ten-lesson course, we discussed many teachings from the Word, but what we most often came back to was "the way of righteousness."

And he was stunned. He had grown up in a church community but had left with only the moral encouragement to "be good." And, comparatively, he was! If he was your dad or brother or friend, you would have been grateful! But he was discovering that God is not just good; he is Good. He is so Good that he can't be reached by moral efforts or behavioral comparisons. So I shared with him another way. John's way. I shared Jesus, "the way." And he believed it!

You can too. You might have spent your whole life thinking that you, honestly, don't stand a chance in hell of going to hell. You may have been deceived into thinking that "their" sins are so much worse than yours. But it's not too late. You too could have a "but later" story. Unlike the Pharisees, "after you saw this" could lead you to the way of righteousness, to the kingdom of God, to the celebration of forgiven sinners. Jesus' story proves that none of us gets it entirely right and that all of us have a chance to change our minds and trust in Jesus. **"This is good, and pleases God our Savior, who wants *all people* to be saved and to come to a knowledge of the truth"** (1 Timothy 2:3,4).

I saw Mark in church last Sunday. I'm still praying that he accepts my invitation to talk so we can sit down with his backpack and my Bible and talk about heaven and hell. Maybe I'll tell him a little story about a father and his two sons and about the way that anyone can be right with God.

STUDY QUESTIONS

1. Which of the two sons is most like you? Do you relate more with "tax collectors and prostitutes" (sinners with obviously messy pasts) or with the religious leaders of Jesus' day (outwardly decent people who, nevertheless, had plenty of sins in their hearts)? Explain your answer.

2. Read Jesus' famous story about the prodigal son and his stubborn brother in Luke 15:11–32. Find at least four connections between that story and the parable from this chapter (hint: there are lots!).

3. Agree/Disagree: Based on Jesus' story, a church's health isn't based on how many people show up on Sunday but rather what those people do on Monday.

4. Meditate on Jesus' words in Matthew 7:21–23. In what ways were the first-century religious leaders like the "evildoers" described here? How does John 6:29 help you answer that question?

5. Do you know anyone who thinks it is too late to be part of God's family? Share this book with them so they could become the next "tax collector" in the kingdom of God!

CHAPTER 10

INVITE GOD INTO YOUR FINANCES

Do you love it—I mean LOVE it—when the church talks about money? Yeah, I get that. Off-putting experiences with the church and money are unfortunately common. My dad grew up in a church where they posted the church offering "standings" on the wall. As a big, poor farm family, the Novotnys never made it too far up the list, and the whole church community was aware of the fact. Disgusting, isn't it?

I once visited a church where the preacher had zero—count them, zero!—words about God's forgiveness and love, but every after-church announcement was about . . . you guessed it . . . money. Lots of us have been guilted, shamed, and scolded into giving, and it makes us a little nervous when the church wants to tell us what "God" says about our money. We wonder if a commandment is being broken and God's name is being misused for money's/the minister's sake.

Not only that, money talk in the church makes us afraid because money means something to us. Money is not just paper; money is power. Money gives us power to enjoy life. We can go out to eat, take a vacation, get cable, go shopping, and live in a safe neighborhood as long as we have enough money. Money frees us from the financial stress of stacked-up bills and spares spouses fights about the recent charges on the credit card. That's why we want money, don't we? Honestly, do you wish you had less money right now? So when someone tries to tell you what to do with your money, even a pastor (especially a pastor?), you naturally get defensive. So much is at stake.

But I have to be real and tell you that I love talking about money in church. I love it like a Packer fan loves a thumping of the Chicago Bears. Here's why—First, because I love the Bible. A few years back, I was curious about this money and God thing, so I went through the New Testament with a highlighter, searching for any mention of money. Giving. Generosity. Gold. Silver. Rich. Poor. Taxes. Treasures. Here's what I found. Out of the 130 two-page spreads in my copy of the Bible, only two didn't have something to say about money. Two! The other 128 had something (often somethings, plural) to say about the subject. It dawned on me that our heavenly Father believes that his children need to hear about money a lot. Therefore, a church talking about money is simply biblical.

Second, I love talking God and money because I love you. I bet money is something you think about, worry about, and pray about, because money affects you in emotional ways. Maybe you had parents you didn't see much because they were working to get more money. Maybe you screamed at your spouse or your own children in the last year because of the stress money was causing. Maybe you disconnected from God's Word for a while because you were making money. Maybe you have been wronged, sued, lied to just to get money. Maybe you've lost your joy thinking about tuition and your mortgage and paying for the wedding. Have you questioned God's love because you couldn't keep up financially? Am I onto something? How could I not bring God's Word to your world, a world where you think about money all the time?

So in this chapter, I'm going to talk about God and money without apologizing. Jesus is going to warn you and me about the "almighty dollar" (interesting phrase, isn't it?). Our Savior wants to reveal that money is often a promise breaker and that only the Almighty God is a continual promise keeper.

Check out Luke chapter 12 with me. **"When a crowd of many thousands had gathered, so that they were trampling on one another . . . someone in the crowd said to [Jesus], 'Teacher, tell my brother to divide the inheritance with me'"** (verses 1,13). Picture the scene. Thousands of people are gathered together, and an extrovert sees an opportunity. There's a money fight in his family, and he wants Jesus to fix it. "Tell my brother to share!" the man demands of Jesus. Has your brother or sister ever said that? "Mom, tell him (her) to share with me!"

Jesus' reply is blunt: **"Man, who appointed me a judge or an arbiter between you?"** (verse 14). "Dude, you think I came down from heaven to settle inheritance cases?" But despite his rebuke of the man, Jesus sees an opportunity. He sees thousands of faces and, as the Son of God, he knows what's in thousands of hearts. Worry. Fear. Stress. Greed. And he knows how much of that is connected to money.

So he says, **"Watch out!"** as if something dangerous is lurking in the crowd. And he adds, **"Be on your guard"** (verse 15), as if an enemy is approaching. Jesus sees a crowd of believers and unbelievers, committed Christians and curious faces and shouts, "Watch out! Be on your guard!"

What's so dangerous? Jesus continues, **"Be on your guard against all kinds of greed; life does not consist in an abundance of possessions"** (verse 15). Greed.

GREED IS THE ASSUMPTION THAT IT'S ALL FOR MY CONSUMPTION.

That's the enemy you need to watch out for. That's the threat you need to be on your guard against.

In my experience, *greed* is a slippery word to define. We have seen it in others, but how do we know if it exists within us? Let me steal one pastor's definition: Greed is the assumption that it's all for my consumption. Greed is when you assume that everything you have is for you to consume.

In this teaching, Jesus warns against **"all kinds of greed."** Consider two forms that greed often takes. First, there is spending greed. "I NEED four bedrooms and eight cylinders and the designer dishes and the top-of-the-line TV and the kitchen cabinets and the riding mower and . . ." Greedy spenders tend to be jealous when others have something they don't. They can't walk through a mall without feeling like they don't have enough.

Second, there is saving greed. "I can't give to this or spend money on that. We can't go out to eat or buy this because we have to save." Greedy savers tend to be judgmental toward people who have nice things and constantly worry about their financial future. But both types make the assumption that all the money is for their consumption. So Jesus says, **"Watch out! Be on your guard against all kinds of greed."**

While that warning echoes in the air, Jesus preaches a confusing story: **"The ground of a certain rich man yielded an abundant harvest. He thought to himself, 'What shall I do? I have no place to store my crops.' Then he said, 'This is what I'll do. I will tear down my barns and build bigger ones, and there I will store my surplus grain. And I'll say to myself, 'You have plenty of grain laid up for many years. Take life easy; eat, drink and be merry'"** (verses 16-19). Sounds about right, doesn't it? We work, earn, and increase our net worth, which leads to an upgraded lifestyle and plans for retirement. About 1,700-plus years before America existed, Jesus described the American Dream.

If Jesus were preaching this parable today, he might have said, "A certain CPA firm was booming. Word-of-mouth advertising meant new clients, which meant new hires, which meant squished office space. So the president leased a new space with more room. Business got even better. Profits soared. He invested well. The market brought good returns. So he said to himself, 'I think I could retire young, spend more time with my family. I could golf every week, maybe twice! I could get out on the lake while I still have my health. I've worked hard. Now I will take life easy; eat, drink, and be merry.'" What would you think of that? Most Americans would say, "Lucky! I wish that was me."

But here's what Jesus says: **"But God said to** [the rich man]**, 'You fool!'"** (verse 20). Wait. You fool? The guy works hard, plans well, thinks long term. What's foolish about that? But Jesus says he's a fool.

Look again at the man's words and you'll understand Jesus' evaluation. What do you notice? What words do you hear the rich man saying again and again? What don't you notice? Do you see it? He says, "What shall *I* do? *I* have no place to store *my* crops. This is what *I'll* do. *I* will tear down *my* barns and build bigger ones, and there *I* will store *my* surplus grain. And *I'll* say to *myself*, 'You have plenty of grain stored up for many years. Take life easy; eat, drink, and be merry.'" I. I. My. I. I. My. I. My. I. Myself. And what's missing? God. The rich man's sin isn't being rich or building barns or retiring early. The rich man's sin is leaving the Father out of his finances.

Jesus then gives the moral of the story: **"This is how it will be with whoever stores up things for themselves but is not rich toward God"** (verse 21). If you're not rich toward God, Jesus says, you're a fool. So watch out! Be on your guard! Beware of all kinds of greed. Keep the Father in your finances. Make your budget with an open Bible. Be rich toward the One who redeemed you.

Two thousand years have passed since Jesus told that story, but it is just as true today as it was back then. There is an idol competing for our love and our trust and our devotion—money. It is a popular god because its promises are breathtaking: "Imagine what I can do for you? Your stress gone. Your fears erased. Your future secure." And so we dream about and pray for more money.

But is it possible that those dollars can't deliver on those promises? Let's examine that question. What was your first job? Back in the day when you first babysat or cut grass or flipped burgers or delivered newspapers, you probably made less money than you do now, right? Your income has probably increased substantially, unless you're out of work. As a kid, $20 was a big deal. Now you might make $20 every two hours. Or every hour! So tell me—has all that money made you happier? Do you have less stress now than you did at age 16? Do you sleep better with fewer things on your mind? Do you feel safer?

But I thought money was supposed to make you

happy! Didn't you assume it would decrease your worries? Do you think people who make more than $50,000/year have no worries, no stress, and no fears? Do you think their lives are just happy smiles and rainbow sprinkles?

Truth be told, money is a good gift but a terrible god. To prioritize money in your life, you will have to make great sacrifices. You will have to sacrifice your time. You'll work and work and work to pay for the house with more rooms than you need and more yard than you can keep up with. You'll sacrifice so much energy at that high-paying job that your brain will be fried, and mindless reality shows and a few drinks will be all you will want after work. And, I hate to say this, but you might sacrifice your family. Years will go by, and you'll miss it. You'll miss the conversations that only happen when you have quantity time with your kids. You'll miss the marriage God wants that only happens through countless dates and intentional effort. And, worst of all, you'll sacrifice your faith. Your career will consume 40, 50, 60 or more hours each week, and you'll wonder why it's so hard to pray for five minutes or read God's Word for ten. Separate from the Word and you'll soon drift from God. Separate from God and you'll be eternally lost. And the sacrifices don't end there. Buy nice stuff and you'll worry about it getting scratched, spilled on, worn, and you'll give up your patience. Pour

MONEY IS A GOOD GIFT BUT A TERRIBLE GOD.

money into the stock market, and you'll sacrifice your peace of mind, worrying about world events, national trends, and struggling economies. Idolize money and you'll sacrifice generosity, the kind of giving that blesses ministries and the poor. It is no accident that Jesus said, "You fool! You sacrificed all those blessings just for money?"

I once worked for a man I'll call John. John was successful. Big house. Latest model of the best SUV. One of my coworkers, a fairly outspoken Christian, also worked for John. He often tried to invite John to church, but John wasn't interested. And one day, John explained why. "Look at what I have," he said. "What more could you give me?" I was just a kid, so I didn't say anything, but his words stuck with me. What more could church/the Bible/Jesus give you? A lot!

Can I be as blunt with you as Jesus was to the crowd that day? For the sake of your limited time on earth, the only family you have, and your precious relationship with Jesus, can I ask you a tough question? Are you rich toward God? Or would Jesus call you a fool? Would Jesus call you a fool because the Father isn't part of your finances?

Here's a quick five-question test to see if you are rich toward God or if you're a fool:

1. Do you believe everything you have belongs to God? Psalm 24:1 says, **"The earth is the Lord's, and everything in it."** Do you believe the money in your pocket is God's money? Do you believe

God is letting you use his car, his house, his savings? In other words, do you believe you are managing God's money like he wants? Or do you think it's yours to do what you want?

2. Do you love God even when you're broke? If like Job from the Bible you lose everything, is God still a good God? Is the only reason you love God because he gives you stuff?

3. Do you give first and ask questions later? Do you trust God enough to give away a generous percentage before you pay a single bill or buy a single thing?

4. Do you love to give? **"God loves a cheerful giver"** (2 Corinthians 9:7). Do you find great joy in giving like God has given to you?

5. Do you worry about money? Do you think that God is so weak that he can't take care of you? Or do you believe you and your money have to secure your own future?

Those are five tough questions. I don't love answering them because I too often act like a fool. I see the tuition bill and hear the stats on how much I need to save for my girls to go to college, and I worry. An unexpected bill comes and teeth grow in crooked and braces cost two kidneys and I can only spare one, so I worry.

But Jesus loves us too much to watch us walk away. That's why he told the crowds, "Watch out! Be on your guard!" Not because he loves to get our money but because he loves to have our hearts. That's why Jesus right here and right now is offering you something money never could. Jesus is offering you real riches.

JESUS IS OFFERING YOU REAL RICHES.

Listen to this: **"You know the grace of our Lord Jesus Christ, that though he was rich, yet for your sake he became poor, so that you through his poverty might become rich"** (2 Corinthians 8:9). Jesus was rich. Where Jesus lived, the paving companies used solid gold on the streets. Jesus' robes made Gucci look like Goodwill. But for our sake, he became poor. Do you know how poor Jesus was? He didn't own a villa in Galilee or a palace in Jerusalem. He once said, **"The Son of Man** [that's Jesus] **has no place to lay his head"** (Luke 9:58). So what did he do? He crashed with friends. Many archaeologists believe that Capernaum is where the apostle Peter lived. And it seems to be the place where Jesus crashed for a few years. How poor are you when you have to sleep on a buddy's couch? How poor was Jesus when he slept on Peter's floor?

But it got worse. When Jesus was killed, everything was taken away. His heavenly crown was replaced with a crown of thorns. His royal robes were stripped, and the soldiers gambled for the mangy robes that Jesus wore. Jesus died dead broke.

"Yet for your sake he became poor, so that

you through his poverty might become rich" (2 Corinthians 8:9). Why did Jesus do that? Why didn't he worship the god of money and enjoy his life on earth? Because he loved you so much he wanted you to be rich. Not rich in man's eyes but rich in God's. He wanted to give you an eternal inheritance, a never-ending life with God that is so good even Bill Gates couldn't buy it. Jesus wanted to forgive you and me of our greed, our backward priorities, our infatuation with money, our faithless worries. And he did. He saved us, not with gold or silver but with his holy, precious blood. And when Jesus rose on Easter morning, he made a deposit in heaven. Peter later wrote, **"[God] has given us new birth . . . into an inheritance that can never perish, spoil or fade. This inheritance is kept in heaven for you"** (1 Peter 1:3,4). We have wealth waiting for us, a mansion in paradise. We have God waiting for us, a Father who will keep us safe from every sickness and sorrow that our money couldn't. We have an inheritance of joy because there will be no more crying or mourning or death for all eternity.

Money promises, "I can make you rich!"

But the Christian can say, "I already am."

Money promises, "I can help you buy the right clothes."

But the Christian can say, "I am already clothed in Christ."

Money promises, "I can make sure people like you."

But the Christian can say, "I'm sure God already does."

If you know Jesus, money can only offer you temporarily what Jesus has already given you eternally.

Do you want to break the spell of greed and be rich toward God? Do you want to be free from the worry, the insecurity, the sacrifices? Invite the Father into your finances. Use God's money in the way he commands.

Here's how we do it in our home. It's a system I borrowed from another pastor: Give first. Save second. Live off the rest. When you get paid, get a gift, get a bonus, get a raise, get an inheritance, whenever God lets you use some of his money—give, save, then live. Pray and plan to give a certain percentage—lots of people choose 10 percent. And give it off the top with joy in your hearts because you know you worship a Giver. It's not only wise budgeting, but it's the key to escaping this idolatry. It can't be all for your consumption—saving or spending—if your first move is to give. One wealthy Christian said, "Giving money away breaks its power. It's like saying to money, 'You are so unimportant to me that I can just give you away.'"

I know you might be scared to live without holding on to every dollar and cent. But don't be. Not long after this parable ended, Jesus said, **"Do not worry about your life. . . . Your heavenly Father knows** [what] **you need"** (Matthew 6:25,32). Your Father in heaven knows exactly what you need in this life (and in the life to come). That's why he gives you forgiveness, love, and, yes, daily bread.

So don't be afraid. Don't worry about your life. Give first. And God, your heavenly Father, will take care of the rest.

STUDY QUESTIONS

1. In what ways has money been a promise breaker in your life?

2. Read 2 Corinthians 8:1-15. How would you describe Paul's attitude toward money/giving?

3. Read Jesus' words about God and money in Matthew 6:19-27. Why do you think Jesus singled out the love of money as the greatest idol we would be tempted to worship?

4. Study 1 Timothy 6:6-19 and connect Paul's words to your life in 21st-century America.

CHAPTER 11

DON'T GIVE UP ON PRAYER

Something my church has always valued from the very beginning is being real. Although our struggles might be embarrassing or taboo or so awkward that you wonder if they can even be whispered in church, we figure as long as you're dealing with it, we want to open the Bible and talk about it.

That's why I want to address an issue that keeps some of us from praying to God like we should, an issue that keeps some of us from having faith in God altogether.

The big question that some of us have is—Why doesn't God answer "good" prayers? I am very aware that some of my prayers are more personally convenient than objectively good. "God, it's my day off, so make it sunny today. God, please, please, pleeeeease let this field goal sail wide right. God, let the Wi-Fi work today. In Jesus' name!" Logically, I get why God wouldn't say yes to all that. What I don't get is why God doesn't always answer good prayers. Morally, objectively, obviously good prayers.

Like when we pray for justice. Justice is that deep desire we have for life to make sense morally, for things to be fair, for all the innocent people to be protected and all the guilty people to be punished. Justice is God's idea, because it's the answer to all the "isms" that make life a mess—racism, sexism, favoritism, etc. That's why we pray for it, right? We don't want a teenager to have to fear for his life while running or driving just because he is young and male and black. No, we want justice. And we don't want people to believe that everyone wearing blue is bad and that all cops are closet racists. No, we want bad cops to be punished and good cops to be protected.

But it's not just social justice. We want justice everywhere else too. We don't want innocent kids to be hurt at home by Dad's anger or Mom's addiction. We don't want the popular and the pretty and skinny and the athletic to get away with murder at school while the humble, kind, and compassionate get mocked and made fun of. We want justice. We don't want good older people who bring the wisdom of real-life experience to be ignored just because they don't know what a TikTok is. Nor do we want good young people who bring fresh eyes and the optimism of youth to be dismissed just because they haven't worked somewhere for 25 years. We want justice. We don't want women assumed to be incapable or men assumed to be idiots just because of their gender. We want justice. In our courtrooms and custody cases, we don't want expensive lawyers or half the truth or a judge's bias or a loophole in the system to determine where the kids end up. We want justice. In every area of life, we want things to be right and fair and just, for innocent people to be protected and guilty people to get what they deserve.

WE WANT THINGS TO BE RIGHT AND FAIR AND JUST.

That's why we pray. We ask the God who sees all of it, knows all of it, and has authority over all of it to do what we can't—to uphold the cause of justice. But sometimes we pray . . . and God doesn't seem to do anything. That's the part I don't get. Why wouldn't God fix it? "God, what's up with that? God, why are you doing that?" Those questions make some of us wonder about prayer. Does it work? Is he even listening? Even if you don't lose your faith entirely, you can lose your passion for prayer.

But here's what I love—Jesus knew this would happen. He knew God's answers to our prayers would test us, would even tempt some of us to lose our faith entirely. That's why Jesus once told a story about this very thing, an odd story about a grouchy judge and a widow who almost punched the judge in the face. If you aren't passionate about prayer, or if you've lost that conversation with God altogether, this is a story you need to hear, a lesson that can keep you close to God even when life seems unfair.

Luke chapter 18 gives us a preview of the moral of this story: **"Then Jesus told his disciples a parable to show them that they should always pray and not give up"** (verse 1). That's Jesus' point. Always pray. Don't give up. Here's a story that tells us why.

"He said: 'In a certain town there was a judge who neither feared God nor cared what people thought. And there was a widow in that town who kept coming to him with the plea, 'Grant me justice against my adversary'" (verses 2,3). I told you the judge was a grouch. He didn't care what God thought, and he didn't care what you thought. When he graduated law school,

ALWAYS PRAY.
DON'T GIVE UP.

only his mother showed up at his party (and even she didn't want to be there). That same judge met this persistent widow.

Widows in Jesus' day were extremely vulnerable. They were often taken advantage of by people who had the means to get away with it. Apparently, one such man, the widow's "adversary," was trying to do just that.

So what did the widow do? **"She kept coming"** to the judge. She knocked and pled, "Grant me justice!" and then she knocked and did it again. When the judge showed up for work, when he was thinking about a case, when he took his lunch break or a bathroom break, she kept coming to him, crying for justice.

What did the judge do? **"For some time he refused. But finally he said to himself, 'Even though I don't fear God or care what people think, yet because this widow keeps bothering me, I will see that she gets**

justice, so that she won't eventually come and attack me!'" (verses 4,5). Ha! The judge didn't want to help her. He was too selfish to care about some no-name widow. But she kept bothering him. She refused to let it go. And before he got a black eye to match his black robes, the judge gave in and gave her justice.

This makes me think of Andy Bernard from the TV show the *Office*. Andy Bernard is one of the more persistent and annoying characters whose personality could be summarized by one of his best quotes: "Every success I've ever had at my job or with the lady folks has come from my ability to slowly and painfully wear someone down." Wear them down. That's what the widow did, and it worked. So what does that have to do with you and prayer?

Jesus knows. **"And the Lord said, 'Listen to what the unjust judge says. And will not God bring about justice for his chosen ones, who cry out to him day and night? Will he keep putting them off? I tell you, he will see that they get justice, and quickly'"** (verses 6-8). Jesus' point is not that God is like the unjust judge—they're both grouchy but you can wear them out if you don't give up. No, this is an argument from the lesser to the greater. If a bad guy is moved by persistence, how much more a good God? Won't God answer the people he chose to be his children? Won't God make sure they get justice? When they cry out to him, when they scream in frustration or sob in sadness, won't he do something about it? Of course he will. He will see to it that they get justice. When Jesus comes back on judgment day, which is sooner than you think, God will say yes to our prayers for justice. Jesus' point? Keep praying.

Okay. I think I get Jesus' point, but my brain has an objection to that. Why does Jesus wait? Why doesn't God just end injustice now? Why do it "quickly" like Jesus says when he could do it now? "Why just sit up in heaven, God, when we're struggling down here on earth?"

Jesus must have known we wouldn't be totally satisfied by this story because, in a rather odd conclusion to this odd story, he said, **"However, when the Son of Man comes, will he find faith on the earth?"** (verse 8). The Son of Man is a nickname for Jesus. The day when he comes is judgment day, the Last Day. And when that day comes, will Jesus find faith? How many people will be waiting? Jesus knows what a struggle this is, when you look around and see the mess and accuse God of not listening, of not existing. Jesus knows that waiting is not our superpower and that we give in to fear, to apathy, to taking justice into our own hands. He knows we need a good answer to that question. So what's the answer? Grab a highlighter—here's the answer. Us. The reason Jesus hasn't brought total justice just yet is us. It's you. It's me. Your best friend. My neighbor.

The other day I had coffee with a young woman who did not understand what had happened to her. "I haven't been using drugs," she beamed. "I don't even want to. And I haven't been hooking up, Pastor. . . . Wait, can I tell you that? And this Bible app. I've been reading it every day. I don't understand what's happening." But I knew what was happening. She was being found. She was finding God. Like a prodigal daughter, she was lost but now she was coming home to her Father, the God who loved her despite all the stuff she had done. Hallelujah and Amen, right?

But did you notice the timeline of her change of heart? "The other day." Ten years ago, she wasn't "found." In fact, ten weeks ago she was still lost. And if Jesus would have come back, I don't believe she would have been saved. So if you would ask God why justice is taking so long to arrive, he would say, "Her. I love her. And not just her."

Every day God is doing that. He says, "Soon but not yet" to our prayers because he doesn't want anyone to be lost. Maybe that's why you're reading this. Maybe you are one of those people who hasn't yet realized the problem with justice. Remember back when I defined justice as "all the guilty people being punished"? That "all" begs the question—are you guilty of anything? We tend to think of ourselves as decent people, not as perfect people but as good people. But justice doesn't care if you're fairly good or better than most. No defense lawyer says, "Your honor, my client did it but he is still better than 64 percent of other people." No, in a courtroom, justice just wants to know, "Did you do it?"

So—can I ask—did you? Did you ever do something morally unjust? Have you ever jumped to conclusions about someone, read between the lines of a text, assumed someone's motives, and reacted with anger?

That means you've punished an innocent person. That's not justice. Have you ever defended a dirty teammate, playing favorites by taking their side? That's loyalty, right? No. That's injustice. Have you ever taken out your anger on someone who didn't deserve it? You were mad about your friends, so you snapped at your mom. You were mad about work, so you snapped at your kids. If you've ever passed on your pain to others, you've committed the sin of injustice. Have you ever had some issue inside—your own worry or insecurity or whatever—and it made other people's lives worse? That's not justice. And if God would come back to judge the whole world with justice, what would happen to you? Maybe Jesus has been waiting for you to see that you have messed up, that you haven't always been a good person, that you need something more than justice.

Maybe he's been waiting for you to see that he is the answer to justice. Two thousand years ago, Jesus came into this world, innocent and entirely good yet willing to die for the guilty, the morally bad. He didn't die on a cross because he deserved it but instead so that we wouldn't get what we deserve. That's what Christianity is all about—Jesus offers us a chance not to get what we deserve. Instead of the hammer, we get a hug. Instead of hell, we get heaven. Instead of God's scowl, we get his smile. So that even if you've messed up a lot of stuff, even if you've messed up all the stuff, you could still be saved. Jesus endured the punishment of justice so that even Satan himself couldn't stop you from being forgiven. So that even if Satan accused you, like a desperate defense lawyer, of everything you've ever done wrong, the cross of Jesus would declare you not guilty, free, free to run home to God and call him your Father in heaven.

That's why God waits. Person by person, soul by soul, he leads us to see our sins and then to see our Savior so we can be safe for all eternity. That's why we trust him. That's why we suffer for him. That's why we wait for him.

And that's why we meet in churches for worship. The message of a God who would wait for us, die for us, that's the greatest. I pray that Sunday after Sunday, until the Son of Man comes, people would find faith.

Soon after we started renovations on our new church building, we put up quite a few security cameras. We've seen some interesting stuff. But our cameras captured something awesome recently. Two guys on the bench outside. One who appeared to be homeless. Pile of plastic bags left on the bench, maybe his only possessions. A guy who looked like he had been through some stuff. But another appeared in the camera on a bike. He talked and laughed and was about to leave before one of them said, "We should pray." So one man sat, the other kneeled, they joined hands, and despite all the pain in this world, in this city, they called out to God. They kept praying.

I hope you do too. Until Jesus saves the very last soul, always pray and never give up.

STUDY QUESTIONS

1. How often do you pray for justice in your community/world? What factors have led you to pray so little/much for this urgent issue?

2. Meditate on 2 Peter 3:8,9. How do Peter's words back up what was said in this chapter about God answering "good" prayers?

3. List three reasons why Jesus is worth the wait, even if this life is unfair and unjust.

4. Read Hebrews 4:16; James 5:16; and 1 John 5:14,15. What other promises does God make to us regarding prayer?

CHAPTER 12

BEWARE. BE WARNED. BE COMFORTED.

A few years ago, one of my daughters asked me a seemingly simple but actually complicated question. We were weeding our yard, rounding the house with our gloves and our buckets, trying to stop the weeds from a hostile property takeover, when one of the girls shouted, "Dad!" I soon found my daughter peering at the ground, examining something green that had sprouted out of the mulch. And that's when she asked the complicated question: "Dad, is this a weed?" By this point in my life, I had cared for hundreds of plants and pulled thousands of weeds, so my brain was prepared for a quick answer to her question. But after comparing the specimen to both its plant and weed neighbors, I wrinkled my nose, raised my voice, and shouted at my wife, "Kim! Is this a weed?"

It's hard to tell sometimes, isn't it? I spent the first

decade of my working life on a grounds crew, planting plants and pulling weeds, and yet I still sometimes struggle to tell the difference between the two. But you shouldn't judge me too quickly. Even the green thumb folks can't seem to decide what exactly is a plant and what is a weed. Some say that any unwanted plant that shows up in your yard is a weed. Others classify weeds as invasive plants that take over habitats and kill their green neighbors. Still others have a separate category for "weedy plants," which makes me suspect that the gardeners are just trying to mess with the rest of us.

So why am I telling you this? Because Jesus once taught that what's true for plants is true for people. We all want to get rid of the bad ones and keep the good ones, but telling the difference between the two isn't as easy as you might assume.

Don't you want to get rid of the bad people? I do. When I hear stories about pastors abusing their power, getting rich off the tithes of poor churchgoers, and preaching purity while practicing adultery, I get angry. "Get those hypocrites out of the ministry!" I think. You probably feel the same way when someone claims to be a Christian but their online behavior is an embarrassment to Christ. Their social media pages are a mash-up of passages, crosses, and angry insults, and the results are ruinous. The world shakes its head at organized religion, and the truly religious shake their heads as the world stiffens against their message. The whole thing makes us mad. We just wish we could keep the good ones and get rid of the bad ones.

I think that's why a young man questioned my salvation. One Sunday, I arrived at church to see a gloomy young man slumped on one of the couches in the lobby. Not recognizing his face, I extended my hand and smiled, "I don't think we've met. I'm Pastor Mike." The young man didn't move. He just glared at my hand, hanging in the tense air between us.

"Are you born again?" he challenged me.

Trying to ignore the rude start to our conversation, I smiled again, "Yes, I am."

He didn't smile back but instead doubled down on his challenge, "Are you *really* born again?"

"Yes, I am," I repeated. But instead of celebrating my new life through Jesus, he launched into a rambling rant about the hypocrisy he's seen at churches whose seats are filled but whose souls are not filled with the Spirit.

While I sensed that our Sunday guest had some mental health challenges and/or substance abuse issues, I don't think his question was all that inappropriate. In our world, how do you know who the true children of God are? Countless stories prove that genuine Christian people mingle with manipulators who hide behind charming smiles. We would love our churches and businesses and neighborhoods to be communities where Spirit-filled Christians represent Christ well, not houses of hypocrisy where Jesus' name is muddied like a welcome mat at a construction site. Thus we cry, "Get the bad ones out of here!"

But, as my daughter found out in the backyard, the

line between good and evil isn't as obvious as we wish it was. In a world where the "weeds" won't raise their hands, what exactly do we do? If Jesus gave you the gavel along with his divine authority, how confident would you feel to judge the living and the dead? (Remember—You shall not give false testimony against your neighbor.)

Confused? Frustrated? Sometimes I am too. Maybe that's why Jesus told a story about this very issue—the parable of the weeds. It's a raw, graphic, comforting, and thought-provoking parable that will help you not to panic when the world is messed up and you can't seem to fix it.

Matthew records Jesus' story in chapter 13: **"Jesus told them another parable: 'The kingdom of heaven is like a man who sowed good seed in his field. But while everyone was sleeping, his enemy came and sowed weeds among the wheat, and went away. When the wheat sprouted and formed heads, then the weeds also appeared'"** (verses 24-26).

One day a good man sowed good seed in his field. Like any farmer, he was dreaming of fruit. Lots of it. He wanted the seed to sprout roots, soak up the soil's food, and go on to produce a harvest that would bless his entire household and more.

But (cue the sinister music) while the farmer and his workers crashed after a long day in the field, an enemy tiptoed onto the property, a pouch slung over his shoulder. Alongside, among, and on top of the good seed, he poured out the contents, the perfect weapon—

darnel. In Jesus' time, darnel was a feared weed due to its uncanny resemblance to wheat. In fact, during the early stages of growth, it was nearly impossible to tell the two apart. Once ripe, wheat would turn brown and darnel black, but before then, the two were identical twins. You can imagine Israeli children asking their fathers, "Is this a weed?" and even experienced farmers hesitating with their answers.

Darnel didn't just threaten the harvest but also the harvesters themselves. Darnel could cause a drunken nausea that sometimes turned fatal, a side effect that explained why only a hated enemy would plant such seeds in his neighbor's field.

No wonder the servants needed to do something. **"The owner's servants came to him and said, 'Sir, didn't you sow good seed in your field? Where then did the weeds come from?'**

"'An enemy did this,' he replied.

"The servants asked him, 'Do you want us to go and pull them up?'" (verses 27,28). The servants were saying, "Before the wheat gets choked out or your family gets sick, we should rip out those weeds, right, sir?"

"'No,' he answered, 'because while you are pulling the weeds, you may uproot the wheat with them'" (verse 29). Despite their noble intentions, the farmer knew that his servants' suggestion was flawed. They would rip out some of the good along with most of the bad. And they might miss some of the bad that looked too much like the good. The farmer wanted better than that.

So he shared with them his plan: **"Let both grow together until the harvest. At that time I will tell the harvesters: First collect the weeds and tie them in bundles to be burned; then gather the wheat and bring it into my barn"** (verse 30). "Just wait," the owner said. "The harvest is coming soon, and the harvesters are experts at their job. They will make sure that every last weed is bundled and burned and every stalk of wheat is gathered and stored. My enemy will not get the last word. You'll see. Just wait."

According to Matthew, Jesus wrapped up this story and launched into the tale of the mustard seed, but apparently James looked at John, "Huh?" John looked at Peter and shrugged. Peter looked at Thaddeus, "You get that?" but Thaddeus had no clue. They sensed this was an important story, but they didn't quite get its meaning, so they did every future Bible reader a favor—they asked Jesus!

"Then [Jesus] left the crowd and went into the house. His disciples came to him and said, 'Explain to us the parable of the weeds in the field.'

"He answered, 'The one who sowed the good seed is the Son of Man. The field is the world, and the good seed stands for the people of the kingdom. The weeds are the people of the evil one, and the enemy who sows them is the devil. The harvest is the end of the age, and the harvesters are angels" (verses 36–39). I love it when Jesus gives us the answer key! So Jesus is the farmer, the devil is the enemy, the field is the world, the wheat are Christians, the weeds are those who don't worship Christ, and the harvest is when the angels show up at the end of the world. Let's break that down.

Jesus is like a farmer, and the people of his kingdom are like good seed. Why? Because he wants his followers to grow, to blossom, to bless the world with the spiritual "wheat" of God's Word. When you grow, you do so much good for others as you share the good news of how a person can be good with God.

The field is the world. All over the world, Jesus has planted good seed. If you think of one country as "God's country," you're way off. Rates of church attendance in Nigeria and Ghana, for example, far outpace those in the United States. The field of Jesus is not Israel or America but the whole world, where he is planting his people so that the final harvest includes as many souls as possible.

The weeds are "the people of the evil one," that is, people who don't submit to Jesus as their King. Those who don't call him Lord, don't give him the last word, and don't repent of their sins. The same ones who miss the spiritual safety of his forgiveness, don't see him as their Savior and don't trust that he is the only way to be good enough for an infinitely good God.

The enemy is the devil. He's not a myth or a rumor but a real being who hates God's Son. Filled with spite, he does everything in his limited power to sabotage the plans of Jesus, which is why he leads his "people" to tempt Jesus' people to have faith in something other than Jesus and love someone more than Jesus.

The harvest is the end of the age (aka judgment day). That day, known only by God, is when the angels will come and sort things out.

What exactly does that mean for you? Here's Jesus' conclusion: **"As the weeds are pulled up and burned in the fire, so it will be at the end of the age. The Son of Man will send out his angels, and they will weed out of his kingdom everything that causes sin and all who do evil. They will throw them into the blazing furnace, where there will be weeping and gnashing of teeth. Then the righteous will shine like the sun in the kingdom of their Father. Whoever has ears, let them hear"** (verses 40-43).

I might summarize the story this way—Just wait. If you are grieved by injustice, just wait. If you ache for good to triumph over evil, just wait. If you cannot stand powerful people getting away with it or help-less victims who have nowhere to turn, just wait. If your family has a story of a struggling Christian being harshly judged by the church, just wait. If you have been wounded by a "holy man" who was anything but holy, just wait. If you are sick and tired of the sick things that are done in the name of Jesus, just wait. The Last Day is coming soon, and when it does, God will sort everything out. Just wait.

So what should you and I do with Jesus' words? Let me suggest one bad application and three good ones.

First, the bad. I don't believe Jesus is telling his

people to "just wait" and not work against sin and injustice. "Well, it's hard to tell who the good people are and who the bad people are, so I'll just wait for Jesus to show up and fix it." While that might seem like a fair interpretation of Jesus' words, that simply doesn't fit with hundreds of other Scripture passages that speak of correcting, confronting, and rebuking those who are living contrary to God's will. Read Matthew chapter 18 or 1 Corinthians chapter 5 or Romans chapter 13 and you'll see that Jesus wants the church to judge and to address sin and wants the government to address injustice. "You shouldn't judge" might sound nice, but consider what that means when a pastor is abusing a minor. "Just wait" doesn't work when it comes to standing up for the innocent and protecting the holy name of Jesus.

So if that isn't the point of Jesus' story, what is? Three things come to mind: Beware. Be warned. Be comforted.

Beware—Beware of your good intentions to get rid of "fake Christians." We all know people who make the rest of us look bad. Like darnel, such hypocrites are toxic to the church's mission of letting our let shine (Matthew 5:16) and winning over our neighbors "without words" as they see the beauty of our Christ-centered lives (1 Peter 3:1).

But beware. In your good desire to get rid of "those people," you might rip out one of God's people, because the difference between the two isn't as obvious as we might like. If Christians no longer sinned, it would be easy. If non-Christians never did anything that was outwardly good, it would be easy. But neither of those "if" statements are true. God's "good seed" still does bad things. And some of my non-Christian friends outdo me in hospitality, generosity, and humility. Your crusade to rid the church of "those people" would cause some collateral damage.

The problem is our inability to see what is within the human heart. Imagine watching me play soccer. Since I am a fierce competitor, I want to win. Badly. And, unfortunately, that drive often gets the best of me, momentarily surpassing my desire to love other people. So when the ref misses the close call, I shake my head disrespectfully. And when I miss an open goal, I give up St. Paul's advice to "rejoice always." From your point of view, I don't look much like "good seed," but what you don't see is my heart. The heart that prayed a pre-game prayer, "Lord, help me be better than last week." Nor do you see me on the car ride home, thinking and praying and confessing my sins to Jesus and thanking him for his grace toward a sinner like me. Nor do you see the message I sent to my teammates an hour later, apologizing for my temporary anger and expressing my desire to be a more loving person. Since you don't see, beware of what you say. Beware of jumping to judgments about the state of my soul. You might not know the whole story.

Years ago, I remember sitting in the living room of a woman from our church whose relationship with Jesus I couldn't quite gauge. She was living with and (based on their kids together) sleeping with her boyfriend, facts that concerned me as her pastor. When I found the courage to address the issue, her reply was . . . confusing. At times, she seemed repentant, a sinner who was struggling to do God's will, just like the rest of us. At other times, however, she seemed flippant, minimizing her sin as if putting God's only Son on a cross was "only human." Later that night, I thought, "I wish people had a Repent-O-Meter on their foreheads. Green if they're good with God. Red if they're not. Then I would know what to say. Then I would know how to judge."

Beware of judging too quickly or too confidently. Beware of assuming you know the entire story. Be faithful in confronting sin and comforting sorry sinners, but beware that you don't rush to do a job that only angels can do perfectly. That's the first big lesson from Jesus' story.

The second lesson is this—Be warned. If you are not a part of "the people of the kingdom," then please be warned. If you are a fairly good person, as good as most of the Christians you know, but you don't submit to the authority of King Jesus, then be warned. Take no comfort in the fact that your life is just as good as the churchgoers you know. Instead be warned by Jesus' words: **"First collect the weeds and tie them in bundles to be burned. . . . [The angels] will throw them into the blazing furnace, where there will be weeping and gnashing of teeth"** (Matthew 13:30,42). Burned. Weeping. Gnashing. If that sounds like fire and brimstone preaching to you, it is.

If you're tempted to roll your eyes at (another) Christian author bringing up the fires of hell, I get it. Maybe you have crossed paths with a buttoned-up, Bible-thumping, pleasure-denying, holier-than-thou preacher (who probably didn't have many friends in middle school) using "fire and brimstone" to force people into submitting to his authority (and give him their money along the way). Eternal suffering is a terribly powerful motivator, and the history of religion is filled with those who specialized in the pathetic art. Some Christians seem sickly infatuated with describing the tortures of hell, stoking insecurities that keep people mentally chained to their churches.

So if your defenses are up, I get it. But before you lump me with that bunch, consider this—Jesus said it. Jesus talked about fire and brimstone. Jesus preached about weeping souls and gnashing teeth. Jesus said that. The same Jesus who told us to love one another, to serve the "least" of humanity, to turn the other cheek, to protect the children, to preach good news, that Savior said this.

In fact, he said it often.

"But the subjects of the kingdom will be thrown outside, into the darkness, where there will be weeping and gnashing of teeth" (Matthew 8:12).

"Throw them into the blazing furnace, where there will be weeping and gnashing of teeth" (Matthew 13:42).

"Then the king told the attendants, 'Tie him hand

and foot, and throw him outside, into the darkness, where there will be weeping and gnashing of teeth'" (Matthew 22:13).

"He will cut him to pieces and assign him a place with the hypocrites, where there will be weeping and gnashing of teeth" (Matthew 24:51).

"And throw that worthless servant outside, into the darkness, where there will be weeping and gnashing of teeth" (Matthew 25:30).

"There will be weeping there, and gnashing of teeth, when you see Abraham, Isaac and Jacob and all the prophets in the kingdom of God, but you yourselves thrown out" (Luke 13:28).

Every bold word you just read is what Jesus boldly said. He said it back then to them, and he continues to say it today to us.

Which means you have a choice—You can either judge Jesus, or you can let Jesus judge you. You can decide that Jesus of Nazareth is a fearmongering preacher whose moral compass is inferior to yours. Or you can admit that fire and brimstone exist because the Son of God said so. Not only so, but he threatened such fire to anyone who rejected his authority as King and Lord.

I don't say this condescendingly. Like Charles Spurgeon, the famous preacher, once told his church before preaching on the reality of hell: "Beloved, these are such weighty things that while I dwell upon them I feel far more included to sit down and weep than to stand up and speak to you."[6] Hell is horrific to consider, even for those who are sure that their Savior-King has saved them from it. So I don't write these words with a smirk on a smug face but rather with a heart that aches for you to turn to Jesus. The end of the story for those who reject the kingdom of God, according to Jesus himself, is unthinkable, but it is not too late to cry out for mercy. This God is able to change weeds into wheat.

Like he did with Peter. English author, broadcaster, and journalist Peter Hitchens abandoned the Christian faith of his parents when he was 15 years old. In fact, to make his newfound atheism known, he took the Bible his parents had given him and burned it in his schoolyard as a ceremonial marker of his rejection of the biblical Jesus. But then, many years later, a painting changed Peter's mind. One day Peter was standing in front of a massive 15th-century painting by Rogier van der Weyden called *The Last Judgment*. As he pondered the author's depiction of the "harvest" that Jesus mentioned in his parable, he noted the happiness of those the angels guided into heaven and the agony of those who were condemned to hell, and something changed within his heart, a turn that led him back to the Bible he had burned years before. Most important, it led him back to the Jesus who was able to save him from the fire he had once mocked and save him for the glory he had previously thrown away.[7]

If you, like Peter Hitchens, have been living outside of the kingdom of God, King Jesus' warning is also his invitation. The harvest is not here yet. There is still time. And, like the tax collector who cried out for mercy (Luke 18:13) or the lost sheep that was found (Luke 15:4) or the rebellious son who came home again (Luke 15:20), God is waiting for you. Come home. The door to the kingdom is unlocked.

Which brings us to our final lesson from Jesus' teaching—Be comforted. Tenderhearted, fearful, anxious Christians who are worried about not making it into heaven can be comforted.

As you studied Jesus' parable, did it strike you just how much Jesus loves his "good seed/wheat"? When the farmer's servants wanted to rip out all the weeds, the farmer refused. Why? **"Because while you are pulling the weeds, you may uproot the wheat with them"** GOD IS WAITING FOR YOU. (Matthew 13:29). In other words, Jesus doesn't want to lose his wheat. Or, to put it more plainly, Jesus doesn't want to lose you.

This is Comfort with a capital C. Our lives, because of our sinful nature and the magnetic pull of the world's pleasures, don't often look that much different from our non-Christian neighbors. We argue just like they do. We push to get our way just like they do. We panic when we can't control a situation just like they do. We sin just like they do. And there are some, in their desire to protect Jesus' reputation, who might wish to pull us up by the roots too.

But Jesus won't let them. Your King will not let you be ripped out of his kingdom. If you have ears to hear (or eyes to read), then find deep comfort in this promise: **"The Son of Man will send out his angels, and they will weed out of his kingdom everything that causes sin and all who do evil. Then the righteous will shine like the sun in the kingdom of their Father"** (Matthew 13:41,43). Jesus is about to send out his holy angels to gather you up and bring you into his glorious kingdom.

"But!" you object, "I do evil too. And Jesus says here that 'all' who do evil will be weeded out. That means I won't make it!"

While I love that you are listening carefully to Jesus, you should know that the Greek for "all who do evil" literally says, "all who continually practice evil." Like the book of 1 John, this is a reference to those who don't repent, who live in sin, who are not sorry for ignoring what God says is good. If you are sorry for your sins and desire to live for God, Jesus is not talking about you. Your sins aren't "continual" but rather broken up by your apologies to our Father. That means that you are one of "the righteous" people he mentions in verse 43 above.

"But!" you object, "I am not righteous. I so often do the wrong thing, so how can I be 'right' with God?"

While I love that you are aware of your own sin, you should know how a person becomes righteous. Listen to the apostle Paul's monumental words: **"Therefore no one will be declared righteous in God's sight by the works of the law; rather, through the law we become conscious of our sin. But now apart from the** law the righteousness of God has been made known, to which the Law and the Prophets testify. This righteousness is given through faith in Jesus Christ to all who believe" (Romans 3:20-22). How do you become righteous in God's eyes? Not by working. Not by your moral résumé. Not by comparing yourself to others. No, righteousness is a gift that you get through faith in Jesus. This is the greatest comfort that Jesus and his friends know and love to share.

Do you have faith in Jesus? I do too. Do you believe that he died for your sins and rose from the dead? I do too. Then we are right with God. We are the "wheat" that Jesus promises to protect. And we will shine like the sun itself when the Son lights up the sky on judgment day. We may not be there just yet, but we will be. Just wait. You'll see.

Put this all together, and you see why Jesus is the master teacher. In this short story, he tells us to beware, be warned, and be comforted by the coming judgment. Not bad for 15 verses!

Years ago I was stuck at LaGuardia Airport in New York. I don't remember where I was flying from, but I do recall where I was attempting to fly to—home. Except home was far away, and the airline wasn't giving us any good news. If we passengers had known how many delays we had in store, we might have saved up some of our complaints instead of expressing them after the first announcement. It was brutal. Annoyed travelers paced and stretched and laid down on the tile mattress of the airport gate as minutes turned into hours. Ornery kids cried, their expressions matched by exhausted parents out of ideas for entertaining their children. But then the hour came. The flight finally boarded. We made it home. We just had to wait.

Jesus has promised you the same. The flight to your true home often takes much longer than you imagine, and the frustrations of life in a sinful world exhaust you. But Jesus, the master teacher, has promised the hour is coming for his people when their weeping will end and their glorious future will begin. Hang on, fellow believer! You are almost home! Just wait.

STUDY QUESTIONS

1. We live in a culture of instant gratification. How might people struggle with this particular teaching of Jesus? Do you? Why or why not?

2. Do you think it is easy to tell who is a Christian at your school, at your job, or in your family? Why or why not? Does Jesus' story make you rethink your assumptions?

3. Were you surprised by how often Jesus mentioned the "weeping and gnashing of teeth" in his teaching? Given the frequency of that language, what does your answer tell you about the kind of Christianity you have been connected to in recent years?

4. Of the three concluding points (1. Beware, 2. Be warned, 3. Be comforted), which impacted you the most? How will your life be different this week if you take this chapter to heart?

5. Check out Jesus' words in Revelation 2:8-11. What encouragement do you find for Christians who are suffering and aching for their pain to end?

CHAPTER 13

DON'T WORRY; HE'S WORTHY

In 2010 Forrest Fenn hid his million-dollar treasure. Fenn was a wealthy art gallery owner, but when terminal cancer showed up, he decided to add some adventure to the last years of his life. So he took a 12th-century engraved bronze box, filled it with gold coins, gems, and precious jewelry, and hid it somewhere in the Rocky Mountains. Soon after, he self-published a book that contained clues that would lead to the treasure. The hunt became a sensation that would consume the thoughts of thousands of treasure hunters and end the lives of at least five men. Jeff Murphy of Illinois fell 500 feet down a cliff at Yellowstone and died. Eric Ashby's raft overturned on the Arkansas River and he died. A pastor from Colorado was found on the shore of the Rio Grande. Rumors raged online. Some even called the whole thing a hoax. Until June 6, 2020. On a Saturday in the middle of the pandemic, a 32-year-old medical student from Michigan named Jack Stuef found Forrest Fenn's treasure, a 10" x 10" x 5" box that instantly made him a millionaire.

Amazing, right? There's something about treasure that grabs us. Buried treasure. Treasure maps. Like Nicholas Cage in the movie *National Treasure*. It makes your heart thump to think about finding something that could instantly change your life. Just the thought is a thrill, not because it's easy but because the treasure is worthy.

That's something you need to know about Jesus. Because following Jesus is not easy. Jesus himself was upfront about that fact. He often said things like you have to "lose your life" or "deny yourself" or "take up your cross" to follow him. He doesn't want a bit of your time or a bit **HE WANTS YOU. ALL OF YOU.** of your money; he wants you. All of you. Your whole heart. Loving what he loves, hating what he hates, and doing what he says is hard. When you pray his prayer, "Father, your will be done," think of what you are asking. "God, your will be done. Whatever you want. You take the wheel, you tell me what to do, you be the Lord, you get the last word, you be the King, and you give the commands. You say, and I submit. You order, and I obey." That is pretty scary.

Think what that means for your life. It means Jesus will reprioritize your time. Any close relationship takes quantity time to talk, listen, and connect. That's true with God. Time to pray. Time to gather. Time in his Word. And it means a whole new way of managing money. Jesus loves to help the poor, loves to spread the gospel, loves the work of the church, which is why he tells us to give before we save and before we spend. And it means the way we treat people changes. Maybe your dad has issues, but Jesus wants you to honor him. Maybe your neighbor is no peach, but Jesus wants you to be patient with him. Maybe keeping your vows is way harder than you imagined, but Jesus wants you to love her, to respect him, even now, especially now. Maybe that member of your family or that classmate doesn't deserve your effort. They take more than they give, but Jesus wants you to love the underserving. And, if all that weren't enough, Jesus wants you to trust him. Trust him with your whole heart. Trust that his words about your gender, your sexuality, your everything are best, even if they feel impossible. All of that (and so much more) is what it means to follow Jesus, to be his disciple.

And that's scary. Some people aren't there just yet. They're kind of interested in learning more about Jesus, about the history, about how he can make them a better person, but they're not ready to surrender, to pray, "Your will be done." Or maybe you are a Christian, but what you're feeling these days isn't the thrill, the joy, the happiness but just how hard this is. The grind of following God. Another day, another try. Another check, another church. Trying to resist (again).

Trying to forgive (again). Trying to be good (again).

If you feel like you're giving up more than you're getting right now, there's a story Jesus wants to tell you. Actually, there are two stories. They are about as short as Jesus' stories go, but they have a big meaning about being part of God's kingdom and calling Jesus your King.

Here's the first one: **"The kingdom of heaven is like treasure hidden in a field. When a man found it, he hid it again, and then in his joy went and sold all he had and bought that field"** (Matthew 13:44). The end. That's the whole story. But it's good, right?

It reminds me of the story of Peter Whaling. Back in 1992, Peter, a farmer from eastern England, lost his hammer in a field. It must have been a nice hammer because he asked his friend Eric to bring his metal detector to help find it. They found the hammer but also stumbled across something else—an old oak chest. Inside was something so good the British Museum now displays it. It contained over 500 gold coins dating back to the Roman Empire, 14,000 silver coins, and dozens of objects 1,500-plus years old. The treasure was worth nearly $4,000,000! And Peter just found it.

That's what happened to the man in Jesus' story. In those days, banks weren't a thing, so many people hid their treasures in the ground. Jesus said one day a guy stumbled across such a treasure. When he found it, he knew it was worth more than everything he owned. So he sold everything he had. He gave up his whole net worth because he had found something that was worth more. And did you notice how he felt about it? Joy. He sold everything he had "in his joy." Why? Because he had found a better treasure.

According to Jesus, that's what Christianity is like. I suppose you could focus on everything you lose, everything you have to give up, all the sins you try to say no to. That's all true, but Jesus focuses on this—Christians have a treasure. We have discovered

CHRISTIANS HAVE A TREASURE.

something better. Just think about what is packed in the treasure chest named Jesus. We have forgiveness for everything we've messed up. Everything! Because of Jesus, God has no plans to get us back. He's not going to sabotage our lives because of our past sins. Nope. Our sins are gone. All of them. And we have love. We are so loved, every second of every day. And best of all, God's love endures forever. It never ends. You can get dumped, fired, cut, overlooked, but you will still be so loved because of Jesus. And you matter. No matter how beautiful you look, how talented you are, or how many people know your name, you matter to God. I mean that. Your life matters to God. Your ups and your downs, what makes you anxious or excited, it matters to him. He cares about you. And that's just right now. Because of Jesus, we get our best treasures in the life to come. Because Jesus went all Conor McGregor and kicked death in the face, we don't have to fear death. A Christian's last breath is the first moment they fully see God. We get to be with God, see God's face, fully feel God's love. No more pain, no more forgetfulness, no more loneliness, no more grief, no more breakups, no more worries or what-ifs, no more addiction, no more regrets. That's what Jesus gives us. That's why Jesus is a better treasure.

Which is why you can sell everything, give up anything, and do it with joy. You don't have to worry because Jesus is worthy. Highlight this: Don't Worry! He's worthy. Don't worry about what you might lose. He's worthy. Jesus is a treasure.

And just in case you missed it, Jesus tells another story with the same point. Here it is: **"Again, the kingdom of heaven is like a merchant looking for fine pearls. When he found one of great value, he went away and sold everything he had and bought it"** (Matthew 13:45,46). This reminds me of that show *Storage Wars*. Ever seen it? The merchant in this parable is "looking" for something valuable like the folks looking for treasure in those storage

JESUS IS A TREASURE.

lockers. And when they see something good, they bid big. They give up lots to get that locker because they've found something of great value inside.

Just like Jesus. He is of such great value that you are willing to give up more than a little time to be in God's Word; you are willing to sell everything, to reorder anything, to seek him with your whole heart. After all, who else offers you eternity? Who else blesses you with unconditional love? Who else makes and keeps such wonderful promises?

I'm not talking about the treasures of this world. Do you know how Jack Stuef felt when he first found Fenn's treasure? After 2 years of thinking and 25 days of actual searching, he found that precious box somewhere in Wyoming. But he made this surprising confession: "I am the person who found Forrest's famed treasure. The moment it happened was not the triumphant Hollywood ending some surely envisioned; it just felt like I had just survived something and was fortunate to come out the other end."[8] Was the treasure worth it? Apparently not.

But Jesus is better. When you see his smile, you won't feel like you "just survived," like you were merely "fortunate"; no, you will sing and celebrate forever and ever without ever thinking Jesus was overrated. Of the many words heard in heaven, *meh* is not one of them, because Jesus is a better treasure, worthy of anything. Worthy of everything.

Don't believe me? Read Revelation. In the Bible's final book, we get a few sneak peeks of what is happening now in the spiritual realm where saints and angels gather around God's throne. One of the more common words heard in that glorious place is *worthy*. In other words, "It was worth it, Jesus! You are worthy, Jesus!" **"You are worthy, our Lord and God, to receive glory and honor and power"** (Revelation 4:11).

So—big final question—how do you find Jesus, this better treasure? In both of these stories, a guy "finds" a treasure. But how exactly do we find the treasure of God's kingdom? Jack Stuef knows. In a post-treasure interview, he said, "I don't want to ruin this treasure hunt by saying it was made for an English major, but it's based on a close read of a text. . . . I understood [Fenn] by reading his words and listening to him talk over and over and over and over again."[9] Instead of getting sucked into internet rumors from other treasure hunters, Jack just listened to the source. To the original. And that led him right to the treasure.

Now that's a slow pitch for a preacher like me. You find treasure by reading text? By reading words? By listening to him talk over and over and over and over again? Ring any bells? Friends, this is why I am so glad you are reading this book. This is why I want you to read the Bible every day, to listen to the glorious things that God has done over and over and over again. This is why God gave us the Bible, so we could find Jesus, so we could realize how rich we are spiritually because of Jesus. And the treasure is right here, right now. For you. Forrest Fenn left a few clues in a poem; our Father just gives us Jesus. Free of charge. You don't have a map but mercy itself. Jesus loves you. He died for you. He is everything you have always been looking for.

It's true; Jesus will cost you. But don't worry; he's worthy.

STUDY QUESTIONS

1. How does doing life with other Christians help you remember the true worth of knowing Jesus?

2. List some ways you can start living out the fact that Jesus is the greatest treasure of your life.

3. Does giving up everything to get the treasure of Jesus mean that you stop having a good life, fun, or nice things?

4. Read what people are saying about Jesus in heaven in Revelation 4:11; 5:9,10,12-14. What do you notice about heaven's songs?

CONCLUSION

This book may be nearly over, but I pray that Jesus' stories will stick around in your heart for a while, just like my pastor's story about the man on the cruise ship with his balloons has stuck with me for all these years.

So when you feel like church isn't doing you any good, remember the farmer who went out to sow seed on good soil and had to wait before the harvest came.

When you are tempted to believe that your prayers aren't making a difference, remember the persistent widow who refused to be quiet until she saw justice with her own eyes.

When you sense bitterness taking root in your heart, remember the servant who was forgiven the unbelievable debt he owed to the king.

When you feel absolutely unworthy of God's love, remember the prodigal son and the sight of his father racing down the road, embracing his child, and throwing together a celebration of grace.

Remember the stories that Jesus told and you will see things that others cannot see—Grace. Truth. The kingdom. The King.

"Whoever has ears, let them hear" (Matthew 13:9).

NOTES

1 Justin Taylor, "How the Snowpocalypse of 1850 Led to Spurgeon's Conversion 164 Years Ago Today," *TGC U.S. Edition*, January 6, 2014, https://www.thegospelcoalition.org/blogs/justin-taylor/charles-spurgeons-conversion-in-a-primitive-methodist-chapel/ (accessed 3/27/2022).

2 Andy Stanley, *Visioneering* (Colorado Springs: Multnomah Books, 1999), 51-55.

3 Jean M. Twenge, PhD, *iGen: Why Today's Super-Connected Kids Are Growing Up Less Rebellious, More Tolerant, Less Happy—and Completely Unprepared for Adulthood—and What That Means for the Rest of Us* (New York: Atria Books, 2017), 3ff.

4 Twenge, *iGen*, 128.

5 http://www.city-data.com/city/Appleton-Wisconsin.html (accessed 3/27/2022).

6 Mark Driscoll and Gerry Breshears, *Doctrine: What Christians Should Believe* (Wheaton, IL: Crossway, 2010), 427.

7 Philip Yancey, *Vanishing Grace: Bringing Good News to a Deeply Divided World* (Grand Rapids, MI: Zondervan, 2014), 133.

8 Daniel Barbarisi, "The Man Who Found Forrest Fenn's Treasure," *Outside*, December 7, 2020, https://www.outsideonline.com/outdoor-adventure/exploration-survival/forrest-fenn-treasure-jack-stuef/ (accessed 3/27/2022).

9 Barbarisi, "The Man Who Found Forrest Fenn's Treasure."

ABOUT THE WRITER

Pastor Mike Novotny pours his Jesus-based joy into his ministry as a pastor at The CORE (Appleton, Wisconsin) and as the lead speaker for Time of Grace, a global media ministry that connects people to God through television, print, and digital resources. Unafraid to bring grace and truth to the toughest topics of our time, he has written numerous books, including *3 Words That Will Change Your Life*, *What's Big Starts Small*, *Gay & God*, *How to Heal*, and *Sexpectations*. Mike lives with his wife, Kim, and their two daughters, Brooklyn and Maya; runs long distances; and plays soccer with other middle-aged men whose best days are long behind them. Learn more at timeofgrace.org.

ABOUT TIME OF GRACE

Time of Grace is an independent, donor-funded ministry that connects people to God's grace—his love, glory,
and power—so they realize the temporary things of life
don't satisfy. What brings satisfaction is knowing that
because Jesus lived, died, and rose for all of us, we have
access to the eternal God—right now and forever.

To discover more, please visit timeofgrace.org or call
800.661.3311.

HELP SHARE GOD'S MESSAGE OF GRACE!

Every gift you give helps Time of Grace reach people
around the world with the good news of Jesus. Your
generosity and prayer support take the gospel of grace
to others through our ministry outreach and help
them experience a satisfied life as they see God all
around them.

**Give today at timeofgrace.org/give or by calling
800.661.3311.**

Thank you!

Made in the USA
Middletown, DE
27 July 2022

70062539R00099